THE HAUNTED GUIDE *to* NEW ORLEANS

GHOSTS, VAMPIRES & VOODOO PROTECTION

RORY O'NEILL SCHMITT, PhD, & ROSARY O'NEILL, PhD

Published by The History Press
An imprint of Arcadia Publishing
Charleston, SC
www.historypress.com

Front cover: *Photograph by Rachelle O'Brien.*
Back cover, top: *Photograph by Rory O'Neill Schmitt, PhD*; *bottom*: *photograph by Rachelle O'Brien.*

First published 2025

Manufactured in the United States

ISBN 9781467159784
Hardcover ISBN 9781540299864

Library of Congress Control Number: 2025941131

Notice: The information in this book is true and complete to the best of our knowledge. It is offered without guarantee on the part of the authors or The History Press. The authors and The History Press disclaim all liability in connection with the use of this book.

We dedicate this book to our forever friend Dawn Henry
(April 16, 1977–November 5, 2023).

Dawn always showed up: a ten-year-old's birthday party, a film festival, a baby shower, a wedding, a divorce. Asked, "What can I bring?" or "How can I help?" She literally picked people off the ground and helped them walk again. Said what she believed, especially when others were too afraid. We admired her for that.

Dawn, you gave others the courage to soar. May you float on angels' wings. Keep visiting us in our dreams…

With eternal love and deep gratitude for our family.
Our husbands: Dr. Dasan Schmitt and Bob Harzinski.
Our children: Olivia Schmitt, Rowan Schmitt, Dr. Dale Ellen O'Neill, Barret O'Brien and Rachelle O'Brien.

CONTENTS

AN INVITATION TO NEW ORLEANS

BY MARK ROMIG

Muse with us, won't you?

Invite New Orleans to be your muse. Climb inside your heart and infuse you with her essence.

Follow her whims and delights at every turn.
Hop on a streetcar. Sail your way past the Gothic mansions of the Garden District.
Take shade under the ancient oaks of Audubon Park,
Gaze up at branches dripping with Spanish moss.
Inhale sugary beignets by the Mississippi River,
Morning, noon and night.
Dance your way down Frenchmen Street,
'Til the sun comes up.

New Orleans embraces you. Entertains you. Comforts you.

Let her revitalize you with her melodies. Nourish you with her French Creole delicacies (crawfish étouffée, beignets, fried shrimp po-boys and gumbo. Have I tempted you enough?)

Greetings in New Orleans. Photograph by Sam Blankenship.

You see, the Crescent City is *home*. Home to me. She can be home to you.

Visit her in these pages.

Mark Romig
Senior advisor
New Orleans & Company

GHOSTS ARE REAL

We hear a *pop* in the ceiling, a fork *fall* in the sink, a *bump* in the children's room. Could that just be the old house creaking? Or is it a ghost?

Are ghosts *real*? It's easy to say ghosts don't exist. Don't really walk with us, sit with us, watch us sleep. Don't really open the path. Don't send us subtle reminders. Don't guide. Don't protect. Don't warn.

Dreams are just rapid random firings. Sleep paralysis makes you *think* you see demons, a scholar at Cambridge University explains. Dreams don't actually contain powerful meaning or mirror our souls.

It's easier to believe *nothing* happens when we die. You just *stop*, a nihilist friend tells us. If we just end when we die, who are these ghosts appearing in New Orleans?

It's fun to say: *Don't. Can't. Impossible. Fake.* The deniable seems all the more worthwhile.

Spirits are exciting, electrifying, attractive and terrifying. Why do we want to simultaneously *know* and *not know* about ghosts? Deep down, we must realize that they are who we all eventually become.

Listen, we usually write nonfiction books—American history, art, culture. Ghost books are fantasy, fiction. But what if ghosts are *real*? What if there are parallel universes, a multiverse? What if the city's hauntings are simply a sign of evolution? Passing on, transitioning our hearts, minds and memories out of our physical bodies into some other body. What if we recognize the supernatural as fact, like our friend Carol diTosti says,

Meet Me at the Cemetery Gates. Photograph by Rachelle O'Brien.

"Spirits are non-carnal, non-material…particles and waves of light in another plane of consciousness."

We are creatives, *and* we are also researchers and historians. Our approach in writing this book includes studying Louisiana legends, visiting haunted spaces and conducting extensive interviews. We refuse to believe all people who have seen ghosts are out of touch with reality, imaginative, drunk, high or hallucinating. Wouldn't it be a paradigm shift, recognizing the reality of ghosts? Read ghost accounts from our interviews. Decide for yourself.

We've seen ghosts in New Orleans, suffered in the resounding terror. It's like, suddenly, we're in a pool of water. We can't touch the bottom. We don't know how to swim. So, we doggy paddle, keep our heads above water, wait for it to pass.

Ignoring and refusing to explore the unseen mystical world makes us vulnerable to the *danger* of not knowing. Well, we'd rather explore ghost encounters. Be *armored* and prepared, not ignorant and weak.

FORWARD THROUGH FEAR

THE REALITY OF GHOSTS IN NEW ORLEANS

Ghosts are everywhere in New Orleans. Do they leap out, jump over fences, catch people by their necks, twist them in the air? No, they are far more discreet.

We don't want to tell you anything more about ghosts here than we must—to protect you.

We don't wish to look at another closed coffin. Fear something inside will lift the lid. Or knock on the casket to make sure someone doesn't knock back. (That's what our priest does, just to be sure the body is truly dead.)

Is this how we want to spend our lives? Grinding our teeth? Turning on the lights?

First warning: *don't read further.*

Don't learn about hauntings that could come true for you. Don't participate in the horror of looking in the mirror and seeing a ghostly dark mist hovering behind you. It could be a demon.

Don't read only about bad ghosts in New Orleans. Don't you know they could come back and punish you? Read about saints, holy ones. Do sacred walks.

We swallow hard. Wipe our brow. Should we, your mother-daughter authors, even be discussing these dreaded ghost secrets? Yes! No. Yes—double yes. We are going to take a deep breath. March through the French Quarter ahead of you—these fourteen blocks of packed, submerged ghosts.

Goddess of City Park. Photograph by Rachelle O'Brien.

We catch our breaths. Slow down. Can we live in this state of terror, anguish and uncertainty?

There's no way we can skirt these difficulties. Ghosts defy our need for normalcy. Bring us face to face with impossibilities. Challenge our ability to handle reality.

Close this book if you think you must.

Or relish the terror. Being scared to death means living more. Breathe deep. Face darkness. Eerie sounds. Putrid smells. Charged visions of the dead. Some of them relive their traumas in the afterlife.

How dare we?

We are creatives from the Irish diaspora raised in New Orleans. Our grandmother Vera Malter Nix shaped us with the most terrifying of stories: lepers at the window, ghosts visiting from hell, a one-legged woman ghost repeatedly murdered on the steps. Grandma always ended with, "I hope you enjoyed these stories. And that you weren't scared by them. And you won't be kept awake."

New Orleans used to be very religious. A church for every bar.

Saints fought the devil (Padre Pio, Saint Theresa, Saint Faustina, the list goes on). We're personally terrified to go into the area of evil ghosts and demons.

We are not like Faust, who confronted the devil. Nor do we wish to become like Dante, who descended to hell to confront evil midway through life.[1] We fear the realm of death and horror.

> *Abandon all hope those who enter here.*
> *—Dante*

We are personally Catholic, Episcopalian and Voodooist, raised in this city, filled with brutality and holiness. We take this journey with you from our perspectives. New Orleans is an old city. She's been through a lot—violence and holiness, goodness and evil, condensed life and death.

We come from a line of New Orleans women, equally devout, equally fearful of death, equally believing in life beyond. Grandma Nix slept with three crucifixes on her bedroom door, triple door locks on her brick mansion on South Carrollton Avenue. She had a prayer altar (replete with a liquor cabinet in the wall). Each night, she'd open a velvet-lined drawer of crucifixes and invite each grandchild to select a cross, blessed by the pope, to clutch while we slept.

Pray at the Pitot House. Photograph by Rory O'Neill Schmitt, PhD.

Her daughter had a prayer altar and was a daily communicant. Rosary Nix Hartel, our namesake, was a scholar: valedictorian at Ursuline Academy, holder of two master's degrees from Columbia University (rare for women). Did she believe in ghosts? Yes. Did she also have a life-sized head of Christ crucified by her bed? Yes.

I, the mother (Rosary Hartel O'Neill), live alone most of the time on Royal Street in the French Quarter. I sleep with the lights on.

Royal and St. Philip Streets. Pen and ink drawing by Billy Harris.

I, the daughter (Rory O'Neill Schmitt), am a bit less fearful and welcome visitation (in limited doses), telling ghosts (some—not all), "Come on in." This makes it doubly difficult for Rosary, but for you, dear reader, it is doubly exciting.

Uncle Joey, a philosopher and a seminary professor in Iowa, warned us: "If you study ghosts, you're calling in more spirits." Are we ready for that? Are *you*?

We fear ghosts, but we are personally going to take this adventure with you so we can find out the areas of New Orleans that are most saturated with them.

Dear reader, we're going to prepare the way, exhume all the possibilities of ghosts here. We will ready you for encounters with spirits in our beloved hometown.

Ancient ghosts lurk in New Orleans. You feel them like a weighted blanket. Like the air full of humidity. Like the rain coming again.

PRIMEVAL GHOSTS REMAIN

We live in a deeply fallen universe. Spirits who remain have witnessed more than us. Do the dead possess more wisdom than the living? Probably.

Ghosts can appear as humans, shadow creatures, even pets. You feel the soft tail of ghost kitty wrap around your legs, the warmth of your dead ghost doggy radiating under the covers at your feet. You reach down, touch the prickly coarse hairs on little Ralphie's back. Exhale, fall back asleep peacefully, knowing he's still here.

Generally, ghosts materialize privately in the image of their living flesh when a person is alone. But sometimes, spirits appear to many, like when a poltergeist rushed through our family's Uptown home.

Don't go to haunted places without a holy object, some gris gris,[2] a rosary, crystals or a cross. Make sure, if you enter a spirit-filled space, you have the strength to confront something bigger than you.

Native New Orleanians, we sense ghosts at crossroads. Where realms touch, like Jackson Square, bound as it is by the Saint Louis Cathedral, the Mississippi River and the bloodred Pontalba Apartments. Taste the psychic experience outside the Cabildo, where tarot readers flip cards to predict your future, often accurately.

The next time you stroll through Jackson Square, sipping a white Russian, remember crowds once thronged here to witness public executions. Their spirits hover.

We French Quarter rats revel in the merriment and the joy. Sing throughout the night. Dance in the street. Celebrate weddings, Carnival and funerals with trumpets, tambourines, banjos and cymbals. New Orleans is a party place and a death place. Driving around the city, haven't you seen the bumper sticker "New Orleans: We put the FUN in funeral"?

The French Quarter bulges with tightly packed houses, no taller than three stories, with balconies. Pedestrians. Cobblestone streets. Rain accumulates and dumps into ramparts, floods cemeteries. Locals sail by in carriages and hearses, celebrating before the last ride to the graveyard. Other times, an eerie quietness skulks downtown.

Our mission is to uncover places where the undead still haunt. Discover what is going on in the afterlife.

Some say ghosts linger in an intermediate state before continuing their journey to the next realm. Is a ghost just the soul of a person visiting for a reason? What unfinished business chains them to New Orleans?

A New Orleans Ghost Tale: Dead on Repeat

For Halloween, I dressed up as a witch. I went to a party at my friend's beautiful French Quarter historic home, which had just been renovated. The house was gorgeous—it even had a chandelier in the bathroom. I was in awe of this place.

The party continued into the courtyard. Something startled me. I looked up to the second-story balcony. I saw a ghost woman, wearing a tignon. She was covered in mud. Her clothes were muddy. Her shoes were muddy. She was surprised when she saw me. She gave me this look like: "You shouldn't see me."

She became very frantic. Suddenly, she hung herself on that balcony. And then, it was like she was on repeat. Over and over again—she kept hanging herself. It was horrifying. I left the party.

That night and the week after, this ghost woman visited me in my dreams. She told me that she hung herself because someone had accused her of stealing. But she didn't. These were her things, and she hid them in the courtyard garden.

Later, I asked my friend from the party, "Did you find anything in the garden when you renovated?" "Yes. We found a little satchel in the courtyard."

These were the ghost woman's personal things.

Sometimes, in a stalemate or in agonizing grief, ghosts manifest. Have you wanted to see these mysterious invisible or "slightly visible" things? The appearance of a spirit makes us question our sanity and invites others to question our credibility.

Why would ancestors want to contact us? Are they calling us over? Are these ancient ones warning us? Coming back for something or someone?

Who are the malevolent ghosts, and who are the good ones? Are these voices emanating from our subconscious, sharing aberrant messages?

Primeval ghosts terrify because we fear they possess more power, having gone through death. Are they really in as much control as we imagine? Do ghosts flit around with very little agency, unable to accomplish anything except basically watch and creep. Through great effort, ghosts might contact a living person—but just barely.

Why all the fright? Because ghosts represent *the end*. We don't want to imagine slipping to the other side, sinking in the quicksand of heaven, hell or someplace else.

We are simply inquirers on this path, hoping to hold on, clinging to our present circumstances. We beseech the ghosts that haunt New Orleans: please don't erupt panic in our lives, lead us to a rash act or a heart attack. We want to keep living, pretty please.

TREAD LIGHTLY WITH US. STAY CLOSE.

Hold our hands as we explore haunted places stalked by the dead—mythic spots, where ancestors rest in aboveground tombs that defy the rain with angels, crucifixes and statues of Christ ascending.

Terrifying hauntings persist in New Orleans. Our mission is to inhabit local spots where ghosts sidestep. *Live* to tell about it.

Experience the mysticism and magic of New Orleans, but we warn you: *be prepared*.

LaLaurie Mansion—Don't Get Too Close. Photograph by Rachelle O'Brien.

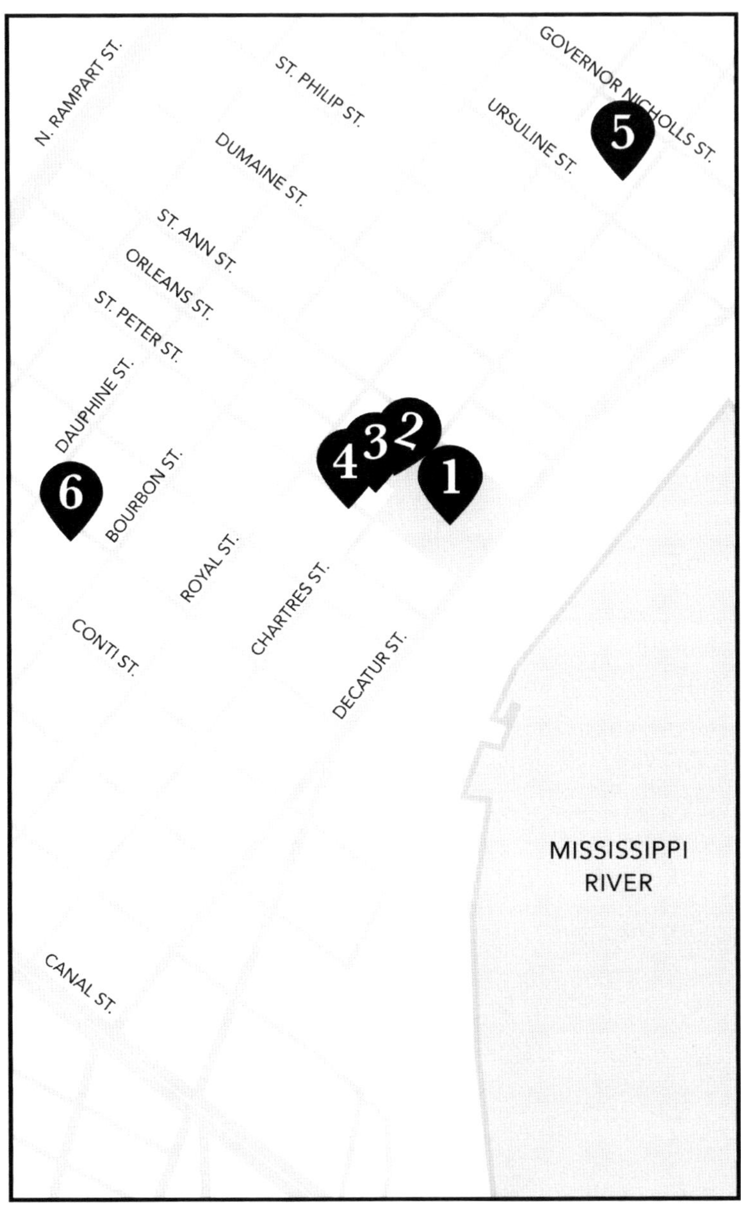

1 Jackson Square, 701 Decatur Street
2 St. Louis Cathedral, 615 Pere Antoine Alley
3 The Cabildo, 701 Chartres Street
4 Le Petit Theatre, 616 St. Peter Street
5 Beauregard-Keyes House, 1113 Chartres Street
6 The Hermann-Grima House, 820 St. Louis Street

1

HAUNTED HISTORIC HOT SPOTS

Everything is so macabre, so hot, wet and steamy in the French Quarter. Strange characters, alive and dead, wander with their ponytails, walking sticks, pocket watches, top hats and fishnet-stockinged legs. Join the spooky world that is always New Orleans after a thunderstorm, when ghostly mist rises from the streets. Suddenly, the sky cracks open and floods the city. We remember that we are always imperiled by nature and what lies beyond here.

Ancient ghosts who have never left New Orleans must enjoy hovering under the oaks and magnolias of Jackson Square. Ghosts feel at home here. Familiarity brings consolation. They see giant crows picking crawfish shells out of trashcans, seagulls winging in from the Mississippi River, thunderous clouds bulging black. They hear the drip on the damp cobblestones from the forever rain. The original part of New Orleans, its center, hasn't really changed. Close your eyes. You'll feel that you're in another century.

We imagine ghosts leer through the fences of Jackson Square, squashing anxious faces between the bars, deciding whether to go in or out or just float above. Maybe ghosts swoop onto horse-drawn carriages along Decatur Street, leapfrog up the levee, inhale the pregnant air of the Mississippi.

Ghosts colonize Pirate's Alley, where illegal goods were once sold at knifepoint. Pirate vessels stalked the river, yards away. Frozen in trauma (either as victims or perpetrators), their spirits remain. Look out for the inconsolable Ghost Bride in this alley. When it rains, you can hear her sobbing. She was jilted at the altar, a humiliation she hasn't overcome. Would you?

Carriage Down Royal Street. Photograph by Rachelle O'Brien.

Happier spirits remain, too. A ghost monk hums songs in Père Antoine Alley. Other phantoms dance on the little plot of grass and trees (St. Anthony's Garden) behind St. Louis Cathedral, lorded over by Christ's extended statue arms. Some snake between the Faulkner Bookshop (yes, William Faulkner lived there) and back to St. Louis Cathedral.

Murder and forgiveness share beds in the city of death.

Keep a light on when you sleep in the French Quarter, ya hear? And if a ghost arrives, be prepared to make a deal.

HOLY MYSTICS RETURNING WITH PÈRE ANTOINE AT JACKSON SQUARE

St. Louis Cathedral is the oldest cathedral in continuous use in America. We imagine saints gaze through those sealed stained-glass windows and behind the cloud-colored walls. The church brings New Orleanians, both the living and the dead, to God.

A fire ravaged this cathedral once, burning it to the ground. When the cathedral was rebuilt (with gracious funds from Spanish philanthropist Don Andres Almonaster), coffins under the marble floor were dug up and put back. Were their souls disturbed? Are their ghosts getting up? Getting out? Going away? Or are these spirits of the cathedral clinging to the vaulted ceilings, still connecting to the checkered floors and marble altars?

Who was Père Antoine, whom everyone whispers about? This beloved priest served at the cathedral and was laid to rest here. He counseled Voodoo queens, prisoners and penitents alike. But why does he feel so aligned to the cathedral that his spirit won't leave?

The cathedral bells ring out. Catch your breath, inhale deep. We're going to cross ourselves, say a prayer, see if he suddenly appears on a balcony or on the altar, holding a candle.

Click. Clack. We hear sandals clunk across the floor. We squint our eyes: Do we see a Spanish Capuchin friar, a little man with a beard walking up and down the church aisle? He's wearing his simple brown tunic with a knotted waist cord. His skeletal face peeks out of his long, pointed hood, which falls down the length of his back.

Since Père Antoine's death at the age of eighty-one, untold numbers have seen him here, especially during the holidays. His ghost is easily recognizable, as a portrait of this ascetic priest with sunken eyes hangs proudly in the church.

Why, for goodness sakes, would a monk want to haunt a church? Does he have some bad news to deliver, some strange question to ask? Is he guilt-ridden? Père Antoine refused to ring the church bell because ringing it was forbidden on Good Friday, after all.[3] Is he expiating remorse for all those lives destroyed by fire under his watch?

A New Orleans Ghost Tale: Dead Rising on St. Philip Street

Quarter Queen. Photograph by Rachelle O'Brien.

One night, after ushering at St. Louis Cathedral, I woke up alarmed. A vaporous woman dressed in white was standing by my bed, watching me. Naturally, I had to protect myself from the intruder. I swiped at her with my pillow. She just vanished.

This experience terrified me. I started sleeping with a nightlight, wearing an eye mask to block out sensing the ghost. But I could still feel this spirit coming to my bed, visiting again and again. It's like she lives here.

Finally, I told the ghost, "I know this is your house, and you want me out of here. I know you don't like me when I'm here. Listen, I travel a lot for work, and I'm out of town. You can have the house when I'm gone."

Since then, I haven't seen her. We've come to an agreement.

Is this holy monk haunted, too? In life, he had to lead masses, hear confessions, preside over baptisms, confirmations, weddings and funerals. In death, he keeps busy, moving about, remaining alert for more requests.

VIOLENCE AT THE CABILDO

We zip outside. Take a left and land at the Cabildo.

It's the seat of Louisiana history, the seat where rules were made, the seat where people were pronounced dead, disappeared, murdered, guilty.[4] It's the seat that was stormed by extremist forays, the seat where people, who broke the rules, were killed.[5]

Death as entertainment? We grit our teeth, wipe our brows. Nowhere is safe in this haunted city.

Can you imagine mothers, kerchiefed and gloved, their children in stockings and capes, fathers in trousers and caps watching criminals be hanged? Execution in the morning, picnic in the afternoon.

Do their ghost prisoners clamor for vengeance? Do their spirits ache for closure?

Pause and pray for their tragic spirits in the loaded air before the Cabildo.

Some came to New Orleans and never left. These ancient ghosts, saints and sinners patrol our streets. Among the angels and devils, we seek what lies beyond. Some of us don't want to see ghosts, but we see them anyway. Because New Orleans is a place that keeps throwing in our face: *time is running out.*

Lil' Angel Protector. Photograph by Rachelle O'Brien.

We must push forward. Try to forget death for a moment. There's still so much beauty to be found in New Orleans. Revelry is our birthright.

We step past colorful street performers frozen into statuesque poses in Jackson Square, trying to capture a few bucks. Maybe they'll head across the street to Café du Monde. Here, you can have a café au lait and munch dusty beignets, dripping powdered sugar all over yourself.

GHOST PLAYERS AT LE PETIT THEATRE

Onward, we clasp each other's hands and continue our ghost march. We snake around the corner to St. Peter Street and land in the world of drama. We enter Le Petit Theater (built in 1789) and stay alert to floating orbs and hazy apparitions.

For over one hundred years, actors have entered this place like mystics searching for revelatory connection. They bear their souls and harness the pain inside their characters to lift others up. Many of their ghosts remain (at least forty have been spotted). Spectacular ghosts spin through like phantoms of the opera. They slide over the stage, linger in the adjacent five-star restaurant.

We listen for the boots of the ghosts of Union soldiers marching through the theater building. We stay away from the theater office, where the suicide ghost of a former manager reigns. We turn our heads to see if the ghost nun is watching the performance. Are we, the living, her entertainment?

We search for Caroline, the gorgeous actress who accidentally fell to her death from the rafters. (Was it really an accident?) When she's not prowling the catwalk, she's helping theater folks find missing swords in the attic. If you need help finding a set prop, call on the dead for help.

We grew up at Southern Rep Theatre in New Orleans, had friends in performances at Le Petit. Some encountered ghosts (like Steve). Others didn't (like Soline).

Steve, a brilliant set manager, was literally accosted by a ghost.[6] You see, ghosts *can* hurt you.

Here's what happened: Steve and a couple of stagehands approached the office. But suddenly, he felt a malevolent presence, some darkness lingering on the other side of that portal. He warned the guys, "We'd better not open that door." They ignored Steve, shrugging him off. As soon as they turned the knob, a poltergeist surged through the doorway, slapped our friend's face, split his lip, shoved him to the floor.

Who was this aggressive phantom with the strength to knock a healthy adult male to the ground and the power to incite disbelief and dread in the surrounding men?

Do ghosts communicate telepathically? Listen to your intuition; it is a spirit whispering. Pay attention to your gut. If something or someone is telling you to not open the door, *listen*.

GUNFIRE SCREAMING AT BEAUREGARD-KEYES HOUSE

Take the short jaunt to Chartres Street and the BK House.[7] Keep your mystical eyes poised for Civil War soldiers, their eyes vacant and their gray uniforms bloodied. Does the scent of musket fire sully the breeze? Do your hear gunfire shots and the screams of furious men?[8]

Will we see active ghosts, like "Napoleon in gray"?[9] Some swear Beauregard pokes around at night, looking for his boots. (In death, will we be incessantly looking for our keys?)

Beauregard House, View from Esplanade Avenue. Photograph by Rachelle O'Brien.

A New Orleans Ghost Tale: The Lady in White

A month after I moved into my house in the French Quarter, I saw a ghost woman wearing a white dress. I started to see her more often during Carnival season. We have a big party here, and everybody gets ready for the parades. The Lady in White likes to make herself known during Mardi Gras.

But she is very particular. She does not like certain things. If I hang up art up on my walls that she doesn't like, she knocks it down. Apparently, she can be very mean to people. If she doesn't care for certain folks, she throws things at them. Literally, she threw a spoon at one of my friends. She made a whole shelf fall on another friend. The Lady in White is always listening, always on guard, always ready to pounce. If people walk by the house and they don't have nice things to say, she trips them.

I met the previous homeowner. She grew up in this house. She asked me, "Have you seen her?"

At first, I didn't know whom she was talking about. "Who?" I replied.

She whispered, "The Lady in White. She used to scare me when I was little."

Revelry in the French Quarter. Photograph by Sam Blankenship.

A HAPPY GHOST MANSION: THE HERMANN-GRIMA HOUSE

So much *violence*. How much more of these angry ghosts can we brave?

No, no. It's time for happy, helpful ghosts. Our cousin Eileen reminded us, "There are good ghosts, you know." After Eileen's mother's death, a family friend was startled when he saw her ghost zip up and down the stairs. She buzzed around the home and acted like she didn't know she was dead.

Hope heats our hearts. We trek less than a mile away to the Hermann-Grima House on St. Louis Street.[10] We hear there's a happy ghost. Is she?

Adelaide is a gracious host. She heats up the house on cold days. Wonderful smells, like lavender, may waft in from nowhere when you arrive. This ghost surely makes her presence felt. (Pay attention to *smells* if you want to encounter ghosts. Our friend feels the presence of her mother's ghost when the scent of sandalwood soap drifts into the room for no reason. Paranormal scents can also signify sanctity. Saint Theresa of Lisieux emitted the smell of roses[11] before and after death.)

This is a joyful home during most of the year, but if you visit in October, we warn you: steel yourself to attend a *Creole wake*. You'll enter a darkened room for Mama Grima, who died at the stolid age of ninety-six.[12] Confront her hexagonal wooden coffin, flanked by a large, flowered white cross and her portrait, partially draped in black. Take a mourner's seat. Cool yourself with a black fan.

Take in the death culture around you. Families dim the light for the mourning period. They cover mirrors and portraits of the deceased with black cloth and shutter the street-facing windows. They set a bare dining room table with each place set with plain lavender mourning china, and a single glass. There's no celebration here.

In the bedrooms, drab grieving attire hangs for adults and children. Black beaded mourning jewelry is laid out on a silver tray. Touch the dolls in the nursery, dressed for death. The boy doll is suited in black. The girl doll is veiled and gowned in black. (It probably looks like the widow doll our grandmother gifted us, a one-hundred-year-doll with gray hair and clothed in a long black dress and cape.)

A New Orleans Ghost Tale: Growing Up Haunted

Before you deny that the dead return, let us tell you our own New Orleans ghost stories.

I grew up in a haunted house on Carrollton Avenue. It was a raised 1830s Creole cottage on the streetcar line, not far from the Mississippi River bend. * *Chandeliers hung from laced, fluted medallions on tall ceilings. Antique doors featured cut-glass windows. A piano welcomed you in the sky-blue parlor. Stained-glass figurines shot streams of rainbow light through the window onto the checkered kitchen tiles.*

I'd bumble through rooms that were all connected. Run my hand over history. Trace cracked drywalls, weathered from the pounding of the traffic of cars and trolleys. Listen to the wild banana trees swat my bedroom window during summer thunderstorms. Hold my boyfriend's hand on the front porch swing and watch the streetcars pass.

But I learned that in Uptown New Orleans, the paranormal was indeed normal. Everyone in the family would witness these tiny, odd occurrences. Once, my little sister and I saw our stereo's cassette tape holder open by itself. A cassette tape flew out. We froze, stared at each other.

I said, "Did you just see that?"

She swallowed and replied, "Yup."

Then we returned to playing with Barbies in our pink bedroom. We knew there were ghosts in that house. (She still doesn't like to talk about ghosts or her haunted basement. She's deeply religious, sleeps with a prayer card next to her bed.)

My brother lived upstairs in the attic, which had been converted into his bedroom. He once heard Dad's ice clanking in his glass outside the door. He just waited because, obviously, Dad was coming upstairs. But the door didn't open. So, he swung open the door. No one was there. Dad should have been on the other side of the door.

Another time, we had a babysitter who was watching us while our parents were out to dinner. She called them up and said, "Come home right now." Mom and Dad didn't understand and came home from dinner early. The babysitter told them, "I can't work here anymore. I was in the laundry room, and I looked up. There was a ghost floating there above your washer and dryer."

Our family's earliest memories in our home are branded with ghosts.

* When Saint Charles Avenue turns at the Mississippi River bend, that avenue becomes Carrollton Avenue.

HAUNTED DOLLS

Ancient dolls get passed down generation to generation in New Orleans, becoming imprinted with childhood memories. Some cherish dolls, while others fear them. A friend visited Anne Rice's New Orleans home and saw her collection of exquisite china-faced dolls lined up on a shelf. But we own a less-elaborate assortment. Some are shoved in closets so they don't scare the children. Others are hidden away in the basement so they can't get broken—like the one that got beheaded last summer.

There's something ominous about these antique dolls, as if evil lurks beneath the perfect façade of a smile showing tiny teeth. Their perfectly lace-trimmed white dresses. Cracked cherub faces. Pudgy wooden knees that creek. Human hair in perfect blond ringlets. Eyes that close shut. Tiny wrists adorned with silver-beaded bracelets. Dolls with long eyelashes wearing ivory wedding gowns.

Some injured dolls sit with their arms outstretched, their broken fingers yearning to touch. Other beautiful ones stand tall, everything perfect—except for their missing hands.

Our family's favorite china-faced doll is the size of a three-year-old. She wears a red gingham dress and knee socks—perfectly sweet, except for her hollow eye sockets. Her eyeballs got displaced, fell into her head. And now, they clink like ice cubes when she's moved. (She needs a visit to Gayle's Doll Hospital in Metairie.)

Antique dolls patrol New Orleans. Hover. Creep. Terrorize. Glare at you with their glassy eyes. Faces painted so perfectly, you'd think they would speak.

When we're not looking, will these dolls animate? We wonder: Could a spirit find a host in a doll? Some fear dolls as much as they fear clowns.

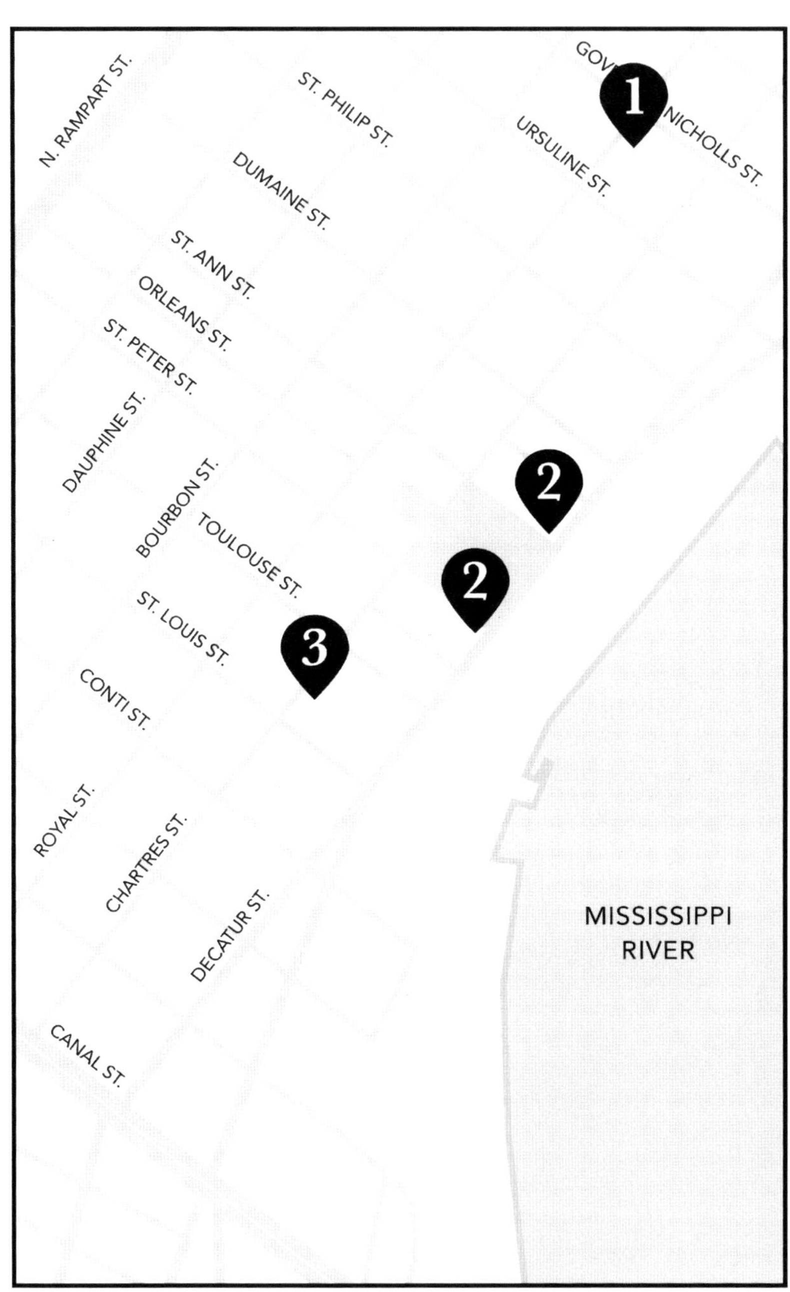

1 Madame LaLaurie's Mansion, 1140 Royal Street

2 The Pontalba Apartments, 500 St. Ann Street and 500 St. Peter Street

3 New Orleans Pharmacy Museum, 514 Chartres Street

2
FRENCH QUARTER HORRORS

Sometimes, I see shadow figures in the French Market.
They go away quickly. When you live here, you see ghost shadows everywhere.
This city is old. Steeped in history and the divine.

Meander the slate alleyways of the French Quarter. Dance on its cobblestoned streets. Absorb the misty presence of those who walked before. Most of the ghosts in New Orleans squeeze inside the French Quarter, those fourteen blocks of historic buildings left over from when the French and Spanish founded New Orleans centuries ago.

The sky darkens, and the lampposts transform into shrouded giants. Careful where you step. All is not well in the Big Easy.

There's *evil* ahead.

TORTURE AT MADAME LALAURIE'S HOUSE OF SIN

Make the sign of the cross when you near Madame LaLaurie's murder mansion. Cross to the other side of Royal Street if you can.[13] We do. Locals skirt this mansion. They fear being sucked into its redone, refaced front. Don't pick up a violent ghost outside her estate. Maybe just a few feet can stop those ghosts from jumping on your back and going for a ride.

Stay clear of Madame LaLaurie's death camp, which you've seen in *American Horror Story*. Avoid her Sharon Tate Hollywood Hills murder house

Ghosts of the French Market. Photograph by Rachelle O'Brien.

in Louisiana. Don't step into her space. You don't want to be contaminated by the violence seething from the ground.

Don't dare talk about Madame LaLaurie—some say. But how can we shut our mouths when we know things? We need to *warn* you, prevent this sort of evil from happening again.

Are you curious about who this infamous woman was?

Madame Delphine LaLaurie (1786–1849) threw lavish parties for other socialites in her ten-thousand-square-foot mansion on the corner of Royal and Governor Nicholls Streets. Prestigious ladies sipped champagne, and well-to-do businessmen toasted sazeracs. And a few worried, "Something isn't quite right."

A burn mark on a wrist, an anxious stutter, a set of hollow eyes. Clues of severe torture prompted an 1828 investigation. Madame LaLaurie and her husband were suspected of cruelty toward enslaved laborers. But the investigation led nowhere. So, cruelty continued.

Her victims couldn't take another day. They would rather invite death by fire and took matters into their own hands. They ignited a heinous blaze on April 10, 1834, and exposed her bloody truth.

Responders raced into the flames and discovered Madame LaLaurie's victims, horribly mutilated, locked inside the attic.[14] There were seven enslaved laborers, bloodied and scarred. Some were weighted by chains, others suspended by the neck, extremities stretched, deformed, dismembered, slaughtered.

News spread quickly. An angry mob raided the house, destroyed property.[15] They found even more barbaric atrocities. Eight bedrooms of misery.

The enraged crowd caught Madame and dragged her out of her carriage. But her coachman took out his *whip*. He thrashed the mob and plunged the carriage forward. Madame LaLaurie got away.[16]

Furious New Orleanians caught up with her carriage and stabbed her horses to death.

Howls echo through the air. Are we imagining things? Screams of the defiant, suffocated ones, those desperate to remind us of Madame's savagery.

An eerie energy surrounds the building. Its evil residue paralyzes the unhoused who try to sleep outside.[17]

Do you dare step past the threshold? Enter this villain's bosom, and you may hear sighs, groans and moans resounding from the torture room. Confront a large man in chains who blocks the stairway and then dissolves into a cold mist.

Brace yourself. Pinching. Hitting. Scratching. Bruising. All from a woman who looks like Madame.[18]

Pray for the souls whom Madame LaLaurie tortured.[19] Humans, once chained up, beaten into doing vileness for the Madame's demonic pleasure. Their spirits were so traumatized, they imprinted themselves on walls, floors, ceilings. Warning you: *get out*!

Who could live here? Someone who appreciates a two-thousand-bottle wine cellar and a speakeasy reached through a mirror. But could they survive the terrors? Since 1834, few have resided here for more than five years. Most are punished. They suffer in strange ways, even after moving out. Health issues. Financial ruin. Insanity. Actor Nicholas Cage declared bankruptcy and sent the home into foreclosure.

Would anyone *dare* to purchase Madame's renovated mansion, undaunted by its racist history? Yes. A ghost entertainment company[20] purchased the building for $4 million (less than half of the listed price). Are visitors prepared to sleep where ghosts moan, where phantom footsteps resound? Isn't the mansion haunted due to the tragedies that were endured there? Architecture can soak up pain and trauma and then proliferate negative energy.

After all, a spiritualist friend shared, "New Orleans is both the light and the dark of spiritual energy."[21]

A New Orleans Ghost Tale: Hurricane Katrina's Guardian Ghost

Hurricane Katrina was headed for New Orleans in 2005. My grandmother was supposed to evacuate with our family. But for some reason, she didn't. At eighty-seven, she'd no business trying to ride out the storm at home.

When we returned to New Orleans, we couldn't find her. Her house in Lakeview had been moved two blocks off its foundation. My grandmother had disappeared.

We looked frantically in New Orleans. Visited refrigerated trucks to identify her body. (The city won't let you declare somebody dead if you don't have a body.) We carried her dental records. Corpses were still being picked up in boats and canoes. But their fingerprints were gone—they'd been underwater too long.

I was still holding on to hope. For my dad's birthday, we went out to dinner in the French Quarter. After dinner, when we got to my car, I noticed this white-haired man, early seventies, propped up on my hood. He was wearing a blue jean shirt and khaki pants.

As soon as he saw me, he called, "Deanna! Deanna, is that you?"

I thought, "Oh, it's somebody that I know." We walked toward each other.

He said, "Listen, I loved your grandmother. I worked with her at Charity Hospital when she was a nurse. I loved her. What a wonderful woman."

Tears are streaming down my face. My family had been trying to not think about this, and now it's staring us in the face.

He said, "I want your family to have closure. I'll give you an address. Go there. That's where you'll find her." He handed me a piece of paper with an address in the warehouse district and walked off. He didn't ask for money. He didn't ask for anything.

I cringed and told my husband, "Oh my God, this is a scam. He's playing on my vulnerability. I'll get mugged."

My husband begged me not to go to. But we went to the building against his wishes. We got there and it was all locked up. So, I called 911. I told them we were looking for my grandmother's body, and the police sent a squad car.

Two hours in, we identified the body of my grandmother. She'd drowned. Her body had been moved to that building, the door locked behind her.

I felt so grateful to that stranger. I didn't care who he was. He had given us closure. We finally knew Grandma wasn't coming back.

A few days later, a detective met us at city hall. Five other families had the exact same story. *Each family was led to different addresses that night and located their drowned family members. Each had independently described the white-haired man the same way in the same clothes to the sketch artist. Everyone wanted to know who this man was.*

The police had access to photographs of employees for the City of New Orleans. With each family, they separately showed pictures of men matching a similar description. Everyone independently picked out the same man. His name was Mr. Sims, and he worked at Charity Hospital.

I asked the detective, "Where do we find him?"

"In the cemetery. He died in 1974."

A paranormal *experience had never entered our minds. This man was 5D. Everybody in my family saw him. There was no question that he was a living person.*

Later, we met Mr. Sim's family. We watched old family videos. The 1974 home video was clearly the man that I saw that night. Clearly the same *man.*

I watched my dad change that night. He said, "We're Catholic. We're not supposed to believe in good spirits. But priests do demonic exorcisms to get rid of evil spirits. Am I shortchanging God—to say that He couldn't send a good spirit to give a message?"

A few weeks later, I met Mr. Sim's granddaughter for coffee. She brought a photograph of him that was taken on the day he died. She covered half of the picture, said, "Look, that's my grandfather in a hospital bed at Charity. The day before, he had been very cantankerous. Had to be restrained. He was clearly not done with all his earthly business. Wasn't ready to let go. But on this day, he had been sung to. Comforted. Reassured that it was okay for him to pass on. That his family would be taken care of. He became calm and collected. He died about thirty minutes later. I thought that it would bring you closure to see who was singing to him, talking to him, holding his hand." Then she removed her hand: "It was your grandmother. There she is in her nurse's uniform at Charity Hospital. She helped him cross over. And thirty-one years later [to the day he died] *is when my grandfather met you in the French Quarter."*

GUNSHOTS WITH MAIMED BARONESS PONTALBA

We speedwalk a few blocks over to the iconic Pontalba Apartments.

Bloodred buildings are wrapped in cast-iron lace. Balconies droop with big-leafed macho ferns. These colossal properties flank both sides of Jackson Square.

Utter the word *Pontalba* in New Orleans, and everyone will immediately connect it to the Pontalba Apartments.

The Baroness Pontalba. *Courtesy of Pierre Pontalba.*

But who was the Baroness of Pontalba? A daughter of New Orleans, Micaela Leonarda Antonia Almonaster (1795–1874) was the richest woman in the city. She inherited her Spanish father's vast estate when she was only two years old. Envy and greed stalked her. Suitors surrounded her like a lake of leaches.

The Baron of Pontalba swooped in, snared her. He partnered fourteen-year-old Micaela with his son in 1811. A magnificent wedding was held in St. Louis Cathedral, adjacent to properties the baroness owned. Did she sense when she left New Orleans and moved into their French château that trauma would await?

Probably not. Foxes are cunning like that. They lure, manipulate, control. The vampiric baron caged Micaela in his family's seventeenth-century château outside of Paris. (We visited the château and interviewed her descendant Pierre Pontalba.)[22] The baron was determined to drip his daughter-in-law dry, wrangle her out of her property next to the St. Louis Cathedral. She said, *no*. Enraged, he attacked her with a pair of dueling pistols in her residence next to the castle. She held her hand over the gun's muzzle and got two fingers blown off. Then he shot her point blank in the chest and left her for *dead*.

The baron slinked back to his study in the château. Shot himself twice. Killed himself. He would never know that after four gunshot wounds, with her fingers gone, left breast mutilated and blood pouring, Micaela survived.

Years later, New Orleans's prodigal daughter returned home, where friends and family awaited.[23] She poured her energy into creating the epic four-storied, red brick Pontalba Apartments, featuring beautiful winding stairs and magnificent high ceilings. Lace cast-iron balconies were emblazoned forevermore with the initials "AP" (Apartments of Pontalba).[24]

Jackson Square Oak, with Pontalba Apartments and the Cabildo. Pen and ink drawing by Billy Harris.

Locals whisper that the shimmering property is haunted. Ancient spirits linger in the Pontalba Apartments on both the upper and lower sides of Jackson Square.[25] Move with caution anytime you stroll near here. You may be clutched in horror.

A NEW ORLEANS GHOST TALE: GHOST GRIP AT THE PONTALBA APARTMENTS

I had first moved to New Orleans, and I was very much into opening everything up. I was trying to set the ego aside and I let everything in, instead of being a little bit more protective. I didn't realize how strong the spiritual energy is in New Orleans. I was just so open and just so loving all of it. I wasn't careful. I walked into a little bookshop in the Pontalba Apartment buildings. I approached a clerk in the back of the store. As I opened my mouth to say, "Hi. How are you?" I felt a hand right on my shoulder. I felt the fingers dig in. I felt the thumb. I felt everything. This force grabbed my shoulder and pulled me back. I spun around. No one was there.

Does the baroness, who was so attached to this property that she lost two fingers to keep it, still prowl the Pontalbas? If you see a woman pacing in the shadows with three fingers, that's the baroness guarding her apartments. Don't try to stop her on her rounds. She's on the lookout for her predator-in-law to come barreling through the door.

Beware of pained ghosts whose terror resounds. Give thanks for good ghosts and for women who changed the world. We don't have to be victims. We can lose our fingers and still fight.

LOVE POTION NO. 9 AND MURDER AT THE NEW ORLEANS PHARMACY MUSEUM

How can we build our courage muscle?

One *rep* at a time. One *step* at a time. One *breath* at a time.

We will not abandon you on this ghost walk. Even if it takes us to *sinister* spaces, like the New Orleans Pharmacy Museum.

We bite our lips and enter the dark shop at 514 Chartres Street. Shadows crawl the shelves, brimming with glass jars and bottles, all packed with rue, wormwood, sage and herbs. The miserably ill barreled under balconies and

New Orleans Pharmacy Museum. Photograph by Rory O'Neill Schmitt, PhD.

galleries and rushed into this pharmacy, suffering from epidemics in the nineteenth century. Could the pharmacist diagnose, treat, heal them?

It was good to be friends with this pharmacist on Chartres Street. Marie Laveau taught the pharmacist here how to make some Voodoo potions. He sold Love Potion no. 9 under the counter, where bottles were numbered so they could be ordered discretely.

A *Love* potion doesn't sound too bad (of course, unless it's a date rape drug). What dark history does this pharmacy hold?

Evil deeds. Dr. Dupas[26] made homicidal drugs in this death shop (1855–1867). If you sniffed a bottle or drank a drop, a seizure might grab you. Murder came in a bottle. No revival.

We're feeling squeamish now. But the back stairs call us to the *murder room*.

The mad doctor hid his lethal practice on the second floor. He performed crude experiments, ripped open pregnant women with lethal weapons, used poisons, cocaine, heroin, razor-sharp drills, knives, bone saws, scissors and scalpels. He tortured them.

No, no. We don't want to see the metal table with stirrups. We don't need to look at the metal collection buckets to believe. We can feel the pain here.

This pharmacy is rumored to be the most haunted place in the French Quarter. When pregnant visitors enter this torture room, some feel nauseated.[27] Others topple from abdominal cramps.

Will we see the ghost doctor, like other visitors? A short, stocky, late middle-aged man with a mustache appears. He's wearing a brown top hat and brown suit under a white lab coat. He opens cabinets, moves items around. When he's angry, he sets off the burglar alarm.

Watch out! He hurls books onto the floor. He shoves people on the stairs.

After the pharmacist died of syphilis, an investigation led to the discovery of the bodies of missing patients in the courtyard.

Ghost victims are trapped here. Look for shadows of ghost children in the back room, where herbs were made. Peek in the courtyard for more of the undead. See if a transparent woman apparition appears.

But there were good pharmacists, too.

The good pharmacists formulated medicines, crushed herbs, minerals, animal parts and insects, blended these into pills, edible wafers, liquids, salves and injectables. They used leeches, opium and narcotics—if required. They could even disguise the odor of death with one of their concoctions.

Our great-grandfather was a pharmacist on South Prieur Street in the Faubourg Sainte Marie neighborhood. Lepers would peer through the shop's window. Their chewed-off faces, swollen eyes begging for mercy.

Grandma Nix told us:

> *One night, my father and my mother were out back, and there was a leper who came by while I was watching the drug shop. The poor fellow, he knew that he looked so terrible. One ear was off. His nose was half gone. Lips gone. I saw this awful person's face in the window. He said, "Lady, I want to buy some things. I only come out at night on account of my face." He wasn't a bad man. He was deformed. He wanted medicines, like syrup and antiseptic. Nobody would give these things to him. I called my father in. He thought something was wrong because I was frightened. (My father knows I never get frightened for anything.) He gave the man all the things he wanted. Didn't charge him a cent.*

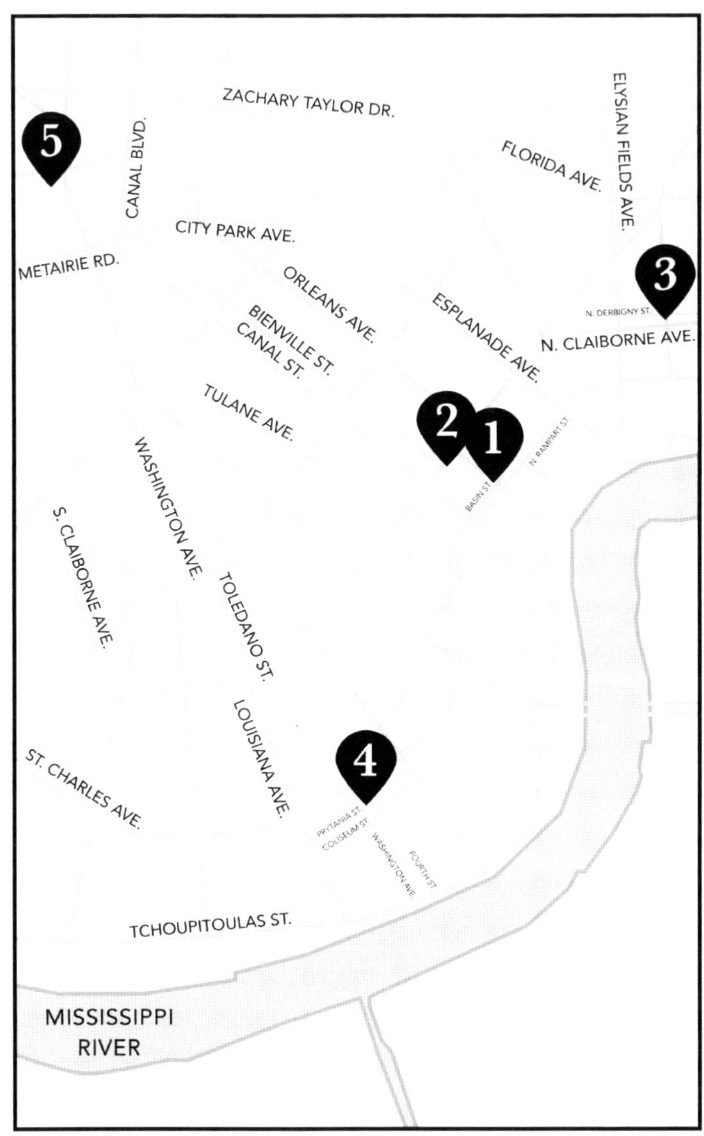

1 St. Louis Cemetery No. 1, 425 Basin Street
2 St. Louis Cemetery No. 2, 300 Claiborne Avenue
3 St. Roch Cemetery, 1725 St. Roch Avenue
4 Lafayette Cemetery No. 1, 1427 Washington Avenue
5 Metairie Cemetery, 5100 Pontchartrain Boulevard

3

CITIES OF THE DEAD

Time is running out. Who knows when we will take our last breath, run a quick errand and never return?

Is our death the final dance? Maybe our souls transition and live on. A departed friend appeared in a dream, saying:

My life is so much easier now.
My life is so much easier now.
My life is so much easier now.

Can the dead visit us in our dreams? Some believe spirits can access you more easily because our brains are shut down for this period. We're in a state of consciousness, and we can better communicate. Our defense mechanisms are quieted down. Spiritual energetic guides (which technically are ghosts) can interact with us in dreams.[28]

Come with us as we meet the dead in our ancient cemeteries, our necropolises.[29] You see, houses of the dead are part of the New Orleans cityscape. Here, we are immersed in a sense of the presence of the past, the company of death. New Orleanians are more accepting of death in a way. Dying seems more natural here.

At our cemeteries, we meet the dead at eye level. Aboveground tombs remind us that corpses are not buried six feet deep in the ground. Bodies remain just behind tomb walls.[30]

Join Us at St. Louis No. 3. Photograph by Rachelle O'Brien.

Forty-two cemeteries creep inside New Orleans. Four million dead in four miles. Their spirits reverberate. It's why we don't feel alone here. You see, some of us never leave.

GHOST RUNNING AT ST. LOUIS CEMETERY NO. 1

One block outside the old city is the oldest of the fourteen Catholic cemeteries in New Orleans, built in 1789.[31] We're hunting for ghosts (and running from them).

You used to be able to visit St. Louis No. 1 anytime. But vandalism, vile assaults and raucous sex acts led the archdiocese to lock it up. You can visit your relatives' graves only if the archdiocese grants a pass. (Our friend Jeff had to prove he was a relative of Edgar Degas to visit his ancestors' tombs.)

Others may enter only while on an escorted tour. So, we arrive as outsiders, chaperoned by an authorized tour guide. Ours goes by the name "Glass Queen." She's dressed all in black—is she in mourning or just Goth? Too early to tell. She shades her face under a wide-spiraled hat. Carries a bat-winged umbrella, always ready for a sudden deluge of rain.

Glass Queen halts. "Wave to the dead, y'all. This bank of wall vaults on your left are stacked graves." She makes a gesture with her hands, "Like filing cabinets, one above the other."

St. Louis No. 1. Pen and ink drawing by Billy Harris.

How many times have we passed these cemetery walls on Rampart Street, not knowing countless bodies were decomposing inside? Crumbling, chipped aboveground crypts, incompletely sealed, house countless family members.[32]

Who's buried here? Nameless babies who died before antibiotics. Others who succumbed to yellow fever, smallpox, scarlet fever, cholera. Corpses loaded in death carts. Lucky ones scored a private tomb. Others barely made the cut-off number in the general plot.

Opposite: St. Louis Cemetery No. 2. Pen and ink drawing by Billy Harris.

Above: Tombs in these Walls, St. Louis Cemetery No. 1. Photograph by Rachelle O'Brien.

We inhale damp air in the teeny graveyard, one square block of a former marsh. We watch out for swamp rats and roaches. The heat is intense. We fan ourselves. Oven vaults block any semblance of a cool river breeze.

Rules govern the dead here. An interred body must be left undisturbed for one year and one day. Their remains can then be pushed to the back—and another body shoved in.

"Put on more mosquito repellent," Glass Queen calls out. "Water gets contaminated in the gullies around the tombs. Mosquitoes attack because of the wetness. Sting your feet, ankles, face."

Glass Queen looks at me (Rory) sporting a short, white lace dress and sandals. She points her umbrella at my legs. "They're attracted to soft, exposed skin."

We shutter. Put our heads down. Keep marching forward, while looking out for snakes slithering in the wet grass.

"The cemetery closes up at night," Glass Queen warns. "Nutria totter about. Large-snouted possums waddle out of shadows, sip greedily from funerial urns. Giant rats soar above—skipping from tomb to tomb."

Four Mausoleums in a Row, St. Louis Cemetery No. 3. Photograph by Rachelle O'Brien.

St. Louis No. 1, Nicholas Cage. Photograph by Cheryl Gerber.

Glass Queen's advises, "Stay close. Don't lean against a tomb wall. It could collapse."

Some grave tops are partially visible, proof that New Orleans is sinking.

We place one foot before the other, pass crypts up and down the aisles, navigate mazelike walkways. We wipe our brows, push our hair behind our ears. Tread lightly. Think happy thoughts so as not to disturb the dead.

Each alley seems to end with another one. Oh my, who knows how many ghosts or savage specters will pop out of their little houses as you pass. Move carefully less you fall into a crevice, step on a hairy caterpillar, get knocked in the mouth by a flying cockroach.

We come to a *screeching halt* at a pyramid, gleaming white, nine feet tall. Our guide points at the inscription, "*Omnia ab uno*. All for one. This is Nicholas Cage's tomb."

Wait. He's not dead yet. "Who would want their tomb waiting for them?" (Not us.)

Glass Queen interrupts, "Don't know. He's *cagey* about it. Some say he wanted to be near Marie Laveau." She spins about.

"All for one." Maybe he wrote this in reference to his *National Treasure* film. Did he hide his wealth in the tomb?

THE TOMB OF THE VOODOO QUEEN

Broken shells crunch underfoot. We follow Glass Queen as she absconds to another tomb. We watch as she gently removes rhinestone hair clips and a votive candle from her pocket. She places them near the tomb. She bows her head in homage, says a prayer.

Glass Queen returns and says, "Marie Laveau. The Voodoo Queen of New Orleans. The most visited grave in New Orleans and maybe even in the world."

We approach the milky pink tomb. (Did Uncle Jay really get hired to professionally paint her grave?) It's fenced off now, had to be protected from visitors defacing her tomb. Some scratched XXX markings all over her tomb (XXX is how Marie Laveau signed her name). Others would break off pieces of stone as mementos.

We say a prayer, read the listing of the eighty-four souls interred with her. Infants, children and adults. Even in death, she embraces all.

St. Louis No. 1, Marie Laveau. Photograph by Cheryl Gerber.

A murder of crows wails overhead. Now is not the time to hear about the snakes powerful Marie danced with in Congo Square. Chanting and channeling helped women grieve slaughtered husbands, carry dead children, try to find some way to reach God. (Marie buried seven of her nine children.)

Holy ones—like a priestess we know from Voodoo Authentica—regularly converse with Marie at her graveside. Seek her counsel. Ask for protection.

Get to know New Orleans Voodoo. See how this spiritual practice invites agency. Lean on ancestors and spirits for guidance. Sing prayers in gratitude to the benevolent God.

Some nights, Marie Laveau materializes. She wears a red and white turban tucked around her hair, brilliantly colored clothes. But as soon as she is spotted, she disappears. God knows how many times Marie's ghost has appeared at night.

Glass Queen beckons us to keep moving. She shares with us accounts of other ghost residents. We are equally intrigued and terrified. No, thank you. We don't want to be touched by invisible hands. Become suddenly sick. Hear voices calling from inside the tomb.

What is that behind us—footsteps? We wait for a disembodied voice to call out, "Do you think they can see us?"

(Glass Queen heard a ghost say this once. When she spun around, no one was there.)

Clouds thicken. Mist descends. Ominous foreboding rises. The sky blackens. Thunder ruptures.

She warns us, "Some spirits like to appear in dangerous places. Vacant, dark areas give them power. Chances for malice." We hear a strange scream in the distance. Glass Queen says matter-of-factly, "The dead cry out if they're unhappy, you know."

Maybe the next cemetery will be soothing. Maybe the rain won't break.

Don't trust that. Daily, a 30 percent chance of rain brutalizes the city, with many inches falling in an hour. The French Quarter buildings have balconies so you can mercifully run under them and not get soaked—but not on Claiborne Avenue, where we are heading.

Glass Queen pops open her umbrella just before it starts to sprinkle—as if on cue. She rages about the massive oaks that stood for centuries, their branches stretching 120 feet, roots spanning 90 feet, brutally chopped down in the 1960s to build a freeway.[33] Countless oaks slaughtered.[34]

BANDAGED AND BRUISED AT ST. LOUIS CEMETERY NO. 2

We step into this bandaged cemetery by a freeway. *Not good.*

An open-aired cemetery is so exposed, unforgiving. Bald lots provide no shade. Vines strangle the few palms that weep and reach out.

Though listed in the National Register of Historic Places since 1975, St. Louis No. 2 barely holds up. (Is it the ghosts here that keep it barely alive?) Structures are crumbling. Tomb doors are broken off. The families who cared for them are gone or unable to make the expensive repairs.[35] Others are dead or disinterested.

We pass sorrowful statues reaching up for God. Monstrous tombs, made of fragile, centuries-old plaster, sweat in the heat. These tombs will crack, weaken, drop.

Glass Queen is full of warnings: "Don't look for a place to sit down or a bench. Everything is collapsing."[36]

When bodies overflowed St. Louis No. 1, No. 2 had to be constructed quickly. Rejected bodies, jaundiced with plague,[37] needed to be interred farther away from the French Quarter—from the *living*. Back then, residents believed diseases were spread by miasmas, odors coming from yellow fevered corpses in the cemeteries.[38]

There was no cure, no inoculation and no vaccination[39] for yellow fever; 150,000 people died from the disease between 1804 and 1862.[40] (In 1855, St. Louis No. 3 was built.) So many lives cut short. So many carts emptying corpses into nameless slots. So many bulging wall ovens sealed. A wall of the dead surrounds the stricken cemetery. Endless bodies stiffen, rupture, decompose inside the wall. Corpses bake so quickly, they disintegrate.

Some less fortunate couldn't afford to be buried in either St. Louis Cemetery Nos. 1 or 2, so their families illegally buried them in nearby yards. A friend of ours in the Bywater uncovered human remains when building a swimming pool. We've heard of other residents who discovered bones buried in walls. Renovations may beautify spaces for the living but disrupt resting places for the dead.

Don't cringe. Diseased cemeteries were pushed to isolated spots.

We imagine some spirits wake up in a place that they don't recognize. They'd certainly be stunned by the roar of trucks on the elevated highway, the busy streets cutting through and the telephone poles gawking down with their crossing suspended wires. Traumatized at what has happened in their hometown. Stunned at what has happened here.

As skies brown with rain, we listen for a ghostly brass band playing a death march. Music fans out periodically from trombones, imaginary and real. Jazz and blues musicians Danny Barker and Ernie K-Doe are buried here, too. Notables, like Oscar Dunn (1826–1871), the first elected Black lieutenant governor who was later poisoned, and Jacques Villeré (1761–1830), the second governor of Louisiana who was ousted from political office, rest uneasily here.

Glass Queen points to a blur in the distance. "Don't be alarmed by a swarm of mist. Could be a baby ghost or violent angry mosquitoes. Their activity increases in the late afternoon. Mid-day sun is too hot. They swarm at sunset and in the darkness."

We brace ourselves for spirits to emerge. Will we spot angels lifting a woman's spirit out her coffin? Will confused Civil War soldiers with zombified eyes stumble about? Will phantom figures float by?

Rumors say there's a bride ghost—fully dressed, with a veil and a long train—who runs out to the street hailing a taxi. Is she trying to get away from these despicable smelly vaults, so damaged by the sun and the floods?

Sunshine shimmers unexpectedly. It's hot here in the world of concrete streets, cement slabs, broken paths.

We pause to check for ghostly figures wandering among the graves, lingering in their walled ovens, pulling moss and weeds from tomb crevices, pushing back loose bricks.

Glass Queen heeds us to listen for whispering between houses. She warns us of a faint wailing that goes on when it gets dark. Unhappy spirits yearn to get out.

Faint knocking sounds come from somewhere. We slash on insect repellent but keep going. If you hear more scratching, it could be an uneasy spirit or just a rat chewing on God knows what. Best to look past the cracked slabs, and doors unhinged with remains exposed.

Glass Queen shepherds us to the exit. Tips her hat. Whispers, "Death is not the end."

WAILING AT ST. ROCH CEMETERY

We leave the rim of the French Quarter. Hurry past Bayou Saint John, with its appearing and disappearing alligators. Careful. Don't fall into that bayou. You'll be eaten alive (like our friend Jeff's dog, who was almost killed by an alligator in City Park Bayou).[41]

St. Roch Cemetery. Photograph by Cheryl Gerber.

St. Roch Chapel. Photograph by Cheryl Gerber.

Next, we visit the Eighth Ward, near Elysian Fields, where Tennessee Williams trapped his characters in *A Streetcar Named Desire*.

Locals flock to this cemetery at 1725 St. Roch. St. Roch is the patron saint of incurable diseases and lost causes. Visitors pray for a miracle at the chapel. Many leave offerings: prosthetics, crutches, plaster casts, bloody rags, harnesses.

Beloved pastor of Holy Trinity Church (currently the Marigny Opera House), Father Thevis, famously pleaded to Saint Roch in a time when vicious epidemics were wiping out the city. The saint answered his prayers. All his parishioners were famously spared from yellow fever. Father Thevis built the St. Roch Shrine in gratitude for saving his German congregation. He's buried before the altar and the statue of Saint Roch. The inscription on his tombstone is mysteriously engraved in Gothic rather than Roman script.[42]

Some say Father Thevis remains here, soaring through the cemetery as a *hooded ghost* in a black robe. He walks through walls. If he feels threatened, he will move through you to escape. Never get between a ghost and its exit, even if that ghost is religious.

Did you hear a barking? Oh no. We won't assume it's a friendly ghost dog. He could be a real dog ready to pounce on us, chew us open! A black hound

St. Roch Cemetery and Chapel. Photograph by Cheryl Gerber.

means death is coming. Will we see the *big black ghost dog*? He's the companion of Saint Roch, the patron saint of dogs. St. Roch devoted his life to the sick and contracted the plague. While he was isolated outside of town, a dog brought him food and licked his sores.

At any time, a ghost could materialize, like that of Henry Vignes, a sailor buried in an unmarked grave. He's a tall, blue-eyed phantom who wanders and asks for directions to his family crypt. We look for another ghost resident, a woman who rises from her tomb, sits a top her grave and watches the sunset.

Does ghost wailing erupt when it gets dark? We won't wait to find out. Careful you don't stumble on poison oak or poison ivy as you dive to run off.

Whispers at Lafayette Cemetery

We zip out of St. Roch and delve into the Garden District. Under the massive mama oaks, we feel the gracious arms of nature protecting us, whispering to us, "Keep going." Luscious grounds and mansions puff with pleasure on Washington Avenue, just few blocks off St. Charles Avenue.

Come On In, Lafayette Cemetery No. 1. Photograph by Rachelle O'Brien.

Lafayette Cemetery No. 1. Pen and ink drawing by Billy Harris.

In the moonlight, Lafayette Cemetery, this temple of death, glows. Gray tombs swell with a sinister beauty, so perfectly captured by Anne O'Brien Rice.[43] It's the cemetery that her vampires visited when they ruptured from the splendid homes of their pasts. (We'll see more vampires in chapter 8.) If you're buried here in the middle of the Garden District, your corpse would be joining the literati and the Mayfair Witches' family.[44]

We enter through the arched gates under the oak trees. We look to our right and left as we notice the rows of wall vaults, 496 exactly. This beautiful Southern Gothic cemetery was filled to capacity with coping tombs, internment chambers, mausoleums, crypts and society graves. Lafayette Cemetery still receives the dead—for a price.[45] Spots to purchase a space in the cemetery open once a year. Plots are rumored to cost upward of $200,000. We've much to learn before entering the death chambers of the "ghost rich."

Dark mystery surrounds us. Grass slides under our feet. Clouds overhead sink to brown, loaded, bulging with dread.

We keep our eyes peeled for our next haunting. A slew of shadowy figures has been photographed here in the cemetery of the "dead rich" (not that the dead rich could be any better than the dead poor). A spirit has been seen descending over the gated fence to pluck fresh flowers off another's grave.

Sullen beauty. We depart before succumbing to the reaper's clutch.

THE WAKEFUL DEAD OF METAIRIE CEMETERY

Rain passes over and the sky lifts. We're off to Metairie Cemetery. God knows this is the last place we want to go. Grandma always said, "We don't want to put you in Metairie Cemetery."[46] Like most New Orleanians, she had a terrible dread of death, only visited Metairie Cemetery once a year on Old Souls' Day to make sure the family tombs were presentable. She never went to a funeral for fear death was contagious.

But death comes for us all. We find our family tombs here, buried on the same tract of land: parents (Stephen and Rosary Hartel), grandparents

Metairie Cemetery. Pen and ink drawing by Billy Harris.

A New Orleans Ghost Tale: The Poltergeist

My brother (fifteen years old at the time) and I (eight years old at the time) were watching television in the living room. We heard the doorknob jangle at the backdoor. That was weird because we had a security door outside this backdoor. It was always locked because we lived in a somewhat dangerous neighborhood (New Orleans had an average of one murder a day). No one should be able to turn that doorknob because the exterior security door was always locked.

The backdoor slammed open. A running blur of energy jolted through the doorway. We didn't even get up; we didn't have time to do anything. A poltergeist ran through the living room, turned and raced through the dining room, laundry room and kitchen.

Dad felt a cold hand tap him on the back while he was washing dishes. He thought it was one of us kids. He turned around. No one was there. Then this spirit opened the kitchen door and slammed it as he left.

This energy shifted things in our home. (Could poltergeists be powered by turbulent adolescent energy?) Chinese paper lanterns swiveled on the kitchen ceiling. The rubber chicken hanging over the stove swung wildly. Every picture frame hanging on the wall was no longer level.

The poltergeist imprinted his mark on the kitchen door, a black rectangle of soot that looked like a burn mark.

My brother recently reminded me: "Just so I didn't think it was part of my imagination: we'd wipe off that soot from the door, and then the next day, it would be back—so much so that I could have friends over and say, 'See that?' And I would wipe it off in my hand. And I'd say, 'Tomorrow, that will be back.' And they'd come back the next day, and that little rectangle of ash would still be on the door. Stayed on the door for a few months before eventually fading away."

Was it an omen? Or a cloak of protection?

(Vera and James T. Nix, the namesake of the Nix Library Branch on South Carrollton Avenue) and a great-grandparent (Dr. Jacob Malter). In death, we all shrink.

Metairie Cemetery welcomes the living and the dead. Family vaults swing open to the once-living. Do relatives rejoice when another corpse joins? Do they shout, "There's room for one more!" Clean-swept aisles and monster tombs glow white. So many sorrowful statues live here. Some weep. Some run. Some hide.[47]

Are there people who plan for and want to be buried in Metairie Cemetery? Well, Anne Rice did. Perhaps the Queen of the Vampires found solace in the statues before tombs that weep, move and mourn their dead. She pulled up stakes from Saint Louis and Lafayette Cemeteries, where her monstrous creatures panted, and built herself a family mausoleum with a black cross on the door.[48] Do the ghosts of her dead vampires come looking for their mother?

Ghost statues shiver here at night.[49] A weeping angel marks the tomb of a young girl, Florence Bridges. This ghost statue cries real tears, particularly on stormy days, mourning the child who died so young.

Will Josie Arlington, Storyville madame, come to life and wander the wide aisles? Do the granite flames on top her tomb ignite into real ones on the anniversary of her death? Some have seen the bronze statue at the door of her tomb leave its post to stroll among the tombs.

We imagine the restless ghost of proud upstart Charles T. Howard kicks about in his center tomb, still furious in death. When the Jockey Club wouldn't admit him, he bought the land adjacent to the track and transformed it into Metairie Cemetery.[50] Charles's spirit patrols the seven thousand tombs and 150 acres he bought. Does he ever venture past the gates?

Do nameless sullen ghosts emerge from their gothic tombs? Do they just accept the fact that nobody is going to touch them, love on them or caress them again? Do they just give up, give in? Or do they rise in defiance?

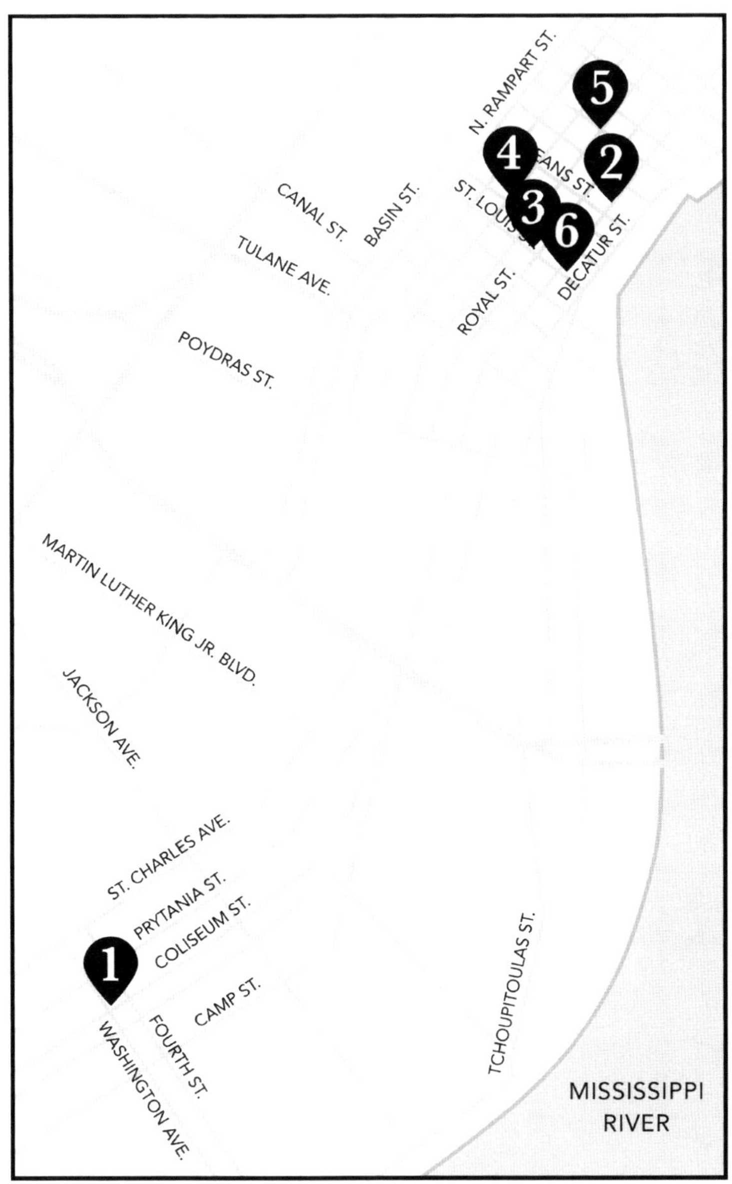

1 Commander's Palace, 1403 Washington Avenue
2 Muriel's Restaurant, 801 Chartres Street
3 Antoine's Restaurant, 713 St. Louis Street
4 Ghost Bar, 605 Dauphine Street
5 Lafitte's Blacksmith Shop Bar, 941 Bourbon Street
6 Napoleon House, 500 Chartres Street

4

GHOST DINING

Our souls demand a respite now. We wonder: Do spirits also need sustenance? Maybe ghosts are drawn to restaurants, too. Crackling crusted cochon du lait, grilled tournedos of black angus beef, bananas foster with vanilla bean ice cream.

The epicurean tastes of New Orleans make our city known around the world. We link arms and walk one foot in front of the other on Prytania Street, wave to Carroll Gelderman as we stroll past Garden District Book Shop. Turn left on Washington Avenue and spot the famous turquoise and white striped awning. Commander's Palace is calling us.

Lightning zaps! Thunder crashes. A sudden afternoon downpour. We dip inside this restaurant and order a twenty-five-cent martini to help face it all.

BRIMMING GHOSTS OF COMMANDER'S PALACE

We slide into this five-star Brennan's restaurant on a Thursday at lunchtime. We request a table in the garden room, where an ancient live oak grows through the dining room floor.

We float past the rainbow balloons. A Newcomb student celebrates her twenty-first birthday. She's sipping champagne, nibbling Ponchatoula strawberry shortcake. Everything in this place screams *money*.

The server passes us black (not white) linen napkins to match our dresses. Can we order courage? No, not on the menu. Andouille and seafood gumbo, turtle soup au sherry, blue crab au gratin, Plaquemines Parish oysters? Yes, please. A few sips of Abita Amber (served in a chilled glass, of course) inject us with just a bit more bravery.

We sit next to an expansive glass wall of windows, gaze out at mama oaks, admire Spanish moss on oak arms stretching to touch us, reminding us that life goes on. One bite of bread pudding soufflé with whiskey sauce emboldens us to face more ghosts in New Orleans.

Behind the satin wallpaper, decorated with dreamy bayou scenes, and past the detailed ivory molding around the shimmering chandeliers, something nudges at us. Paranormal energy vibrates beneath it all.

We ask a server carrying pecan-crusted trout, "Is this place haunted?" He points to Lafayette Cemetery and responds matter-of-factly, "Of course it is. We're located across the street from one of the oldest cemeteries in the city."

Our eyes remain peeled for what spirits may emerge. Will Commander's little girl ghost spook us? She appears and disappears just as quickly, dressed daintily in white. Hardly innocent, she howls, yowls and yips, disturbing the entire floor before she darts up and down the stairs. Children ghosts feel invasive, determined to disrupt. Other times, they are inobtrusive, and we second guess if they are really there.

We look for a mustachioed and properly dressed gentleman—that's Chef Emile Commander.[51] He's dead. Commander Palace's ghostly founder is known to return to check on the perfection of his restaurant's service and cuisine. His guests, the powerful elite, have refined tastes. He supervises Creole crème brûlot and bananas foster, flambéed tableside. He sniffs the aromas (we would) and stands alert as the bartender vigorously shakes a Ramos gin fizz.

The rain lets up, but our curiosity doesn't. We hop aboard a St. Charles Avenue streetcar and head for the haunted restaurants of the Vieux Carré.

THE DEMANDING PHANTOM AT MURIEL'S RESTAURANT

Join us at Muriel's, a candlelit restaurant housed in a mid-1700s brick building near Jackson Square. We order the finest Creole cuisine and a glass of Cabernet Sauvignon and slink into fifteen thousand square feet of luxury.

Muriel's. Photograph by Rachelle O'Brien.

Muriel's, with its cast-iron wrap-around balcony, stretches around a luscious French Quarter courtyard. Careful, a sinister spirit lurks in the shadows.

Delicious appetizers arrive. We take solemn bites of shrimp and goat cheese crêpes and await our *summoning*. The resident ghost may invite us to his private table.

Pierre Jourdan spent his fortune on creating this lavish residence. Then he lost it in a game of poker.[52] No shrimp étouffée or crawfish bread could comfort him. He wrapped a noose around his neck and hanged himself upstairs. His body was removed, but his soul was not. (If you're brave enough, visit this room, the Séance Lounge. Listen for distinct knocks on the brick wall. Do you hear the voice of a ghost reverberating?)

Pierre presides over Muriel's like an enfant terrible. Best keep him appeased, play nice, maintain your distance. Tread carefully if he invites you to sit with him. *Dine at your own risk.*

Tonight is for laughter, celebration, enjoyment. We visit with our friend Anne for extravagance, not a malevolent encounter. Why would a ghost even want to disturb Muriel's, just steps from St. Louis Cathedral?

We hope we can digest the shrimp and grits we've ordered. Will Pierre make himself known by touching us? Leaning over us? Whispering into our ears? Will we shiver when his cold energy hovers behind us? Will we feel his darkness if his shadow passes by?

We are truly *terrified* of angry ghosts. If he feels he's not being respected, Pierre will explode, ransack the building, break things, push over tables, fling glasses from the courtyard bar, twelve feet across to a brick wall, shattering them.

In 2002, a psychic medium spoke with this rageful ghost Pierre and tried to find an agreement that would quell his outbursts. Pierre gave very specific demands: "I want a table with bread and wine, reserved for myself and my guest, whomever I may want to invite every night."

Staff have learned that if such a place is not set, Pierre will catapult glasses and send top-shelf liquor crashing to the ground. In 2018, when staff forgot to bring Pierre his wine, he showed his furor with $49,000 of damages. Windows imploded. The FBI couldn't explain what happened. They deemed Muriel's a haunted house, a classification that just does *not* happen.

We visited Pierre's special table, set with fresh white linen, two place settings and bread and wine. Muriel's honors him in a separate room (just downstairs from where he hanged himself). You may have to request permission to visit his lone table. If you're lucky, a foggy ghost figure will take a seat at the table.

Quick! Snap a picture, and his shadowy outline could appear.

OLD SPIRITS RAGING AT ANTOINE'S RESTAURANT

We hike a few blocks from our home on Royal Street to visit Antoine's Restaurant. Hard to believe this glamorous place harbors the dead. The front room has twenty-foot chandeliered ceilings and giant windows overlooking St. Louis Street. The garnet-red room displays cases of dazzling Carnival

French Quarter Street. Photograph by Rachelle O'Brien.

crowns and scepters. Thirteen more dining rooms glitter with tuxedoed servers and the sugary smells of baked Alaska.[53]

My (Rosary's) father delighted at the king's dinner. He'd look forward to pommes de terre soufflés[54] and steak with marchand de vin sauce and dining with other members of the Rex krewe. Did he ever hear spirits call each other's names in the Twelfth Night Revelers Room? Did he sense a presence as he walked down the hall and leaned over to regard his wife's picture as a maid in Rex that hangs in the back hallway?

We try not to imagine spirits floating through the fifty thousand square feet of interconnected rooms. It's best to just focus on the plates in front of us. We ignore the paranormal mist if it appears suddenly in the corner of the Hermes Room. We sip a sazerac, keep our heads down.

We wait for doors to open and slam without explanation. We take a bite and look for phantoms to come plundering through the room and crash crystal glassware to the floor. Will we hear disembodied voices of patrons socializing in the Escargot Room? We hope so. Some New Orleanians bask in Antoine's glamor in the afterlife.[55]

We don't dare visit the wine cellar, with its twenty-five thousand bottles stacked from floor to ceiling. We don't want to meet the Victorian ghost woman with her child.

Wait. Was that an apparition in waiter's garb moving toward the Mystery Room? Are those two servers who are dashing into the Tabasco Room, carrying Pimms cups and platters of crawfish tails, living or dead? It's hard to tell.

Some feel Antoine Alciatore's ghost rushing before the glass-cased walls of kings' robes, scepters and crowns.[56] Why would the founder, who left America to die in Marseille, come back 180 years later to survey his restaurant's status? Some dark pressure must have been upon this chef. We tiptoe into the Capital Room, the Proteus Room, the 1840 Room, looking for him. Will he appear and then vanish? If we order the oysters Rockefeller, will he swoop in to check on it? Why is this 202-year-old dead man still here?

Julie. Julie. Is that Antoine's voice calling out? Let's see if we can spot him in that corner over there, holding the hand of a beautiful ghost woman.

WRAITH THREATENING AT GHOST BAR

There's so much fluidity in New Orleans. The living and the dead float in and out of French Quarter wrought-iron balconies, luscious tropical courtyards and Creole shotgun houses painted the color of bubblegum. The dead soar above us, blessing and torturing us. We face a storm, a flood, a pestilence of mosquitoes and gnats, scorching heat, all the vile things the flesh can be corrupted by.

It's best to just relax about it on Royal Street. Sip a bloody Mary in the courtyard by the pool with our neighbors Sam and Tracy. Celebrate life while we still have it.

Join us as we two-step down Iberville Street to the Ghost Bar. Here, we can dance till we collapse. Sing till we are forced onto vocal rest. Revel until we start to see ghosts ourselves. Does this bar invite ghosts? Let's drink a Pear Potion (a sour drink with sour gummy worms at the bottom) and find out.

THE NAPOLEON HOUSE: KNOCKING COMING FROM THE INSIDE

You can't visit New Orleans and skip the Napoleon House (owned by our second cousin Susan Gore Brennan). At dawn, the old brick structure is so quiet. Almost feels like you're in church. The dormered hip roof and shallow balconies cry out for a cool bath. The only thing missing is the soft rain.

Built in 1797, this three-story brick building was offered as a residence to Napoleon Bonaparte, but he never made it here. The mayor made it his residence. While he entertained inside, his guards climbed to the cupola for a 360-degree view of New Orleans to watch for pirates coming up the Mississippi River.

Step inside the Napoleon House (now a restaurant and bar). You'll feel you've lost centuries. We dare you to try to look and not touch the puffy muffalettas pregnant with olive tapani that fly out of the kitchen. Or taste the gumbo and red beans, steaming with Creole spices.

Claim respite in the courtyard patio. Sip an old fashioned next to a cherub statue, his lips poised in a smile. Relax as you listen to the fountain trickle behind you. The Napoleon House's antiquated character calls for music, which obligingly drifts in from the Quarter. Songs take humans to emotional places. You sit feeling you have God on your wings and feet that could fly. Music can also work as a tenderizer for ghostly spirits.

Everything hums at Napoleon House with an otherworldly feeling. More *unseen* than seen. What ghosts remain? A photo shoot in the cupola terrified one photographer when she discovered the reflection of a young ghost boy's face in the window. (There were only two women in the room.) Upstairs, a server tells us she's seen a blur of a male ghost rushing past at night. Certain spaces in the reception hall on the second floor thrum with a special energy felt by us. Later, the manager pointed out that a clairvoyant identified a presence in these same places.

But perhaps the scariest part of the haunting is the *knocking*. After the staff lock up the building at night, they frequently hear distinct knocks coming from the inside. It is so clear and so real. It's like someone wants to get out. The staff open the door and check to see: Who is inside? *No one.*

DRUNKEN ASSAULTS AT LAFITTE'S BLACKSMITH SHOP BAR

Our next stop is our favorite bar on Bourbon Street, Jean Lafitte's Blacksmith's Shop.[57] We sense something beyond the visible here. (Some New Orleanians are attuned to ghosts, while others are distinctly turned off.) Our ghost sensor clicks *on*. A knowing feeling erupts. Beings beyond what we can see inhabit every crevice.

An ancient building, built between 1722 and 1723, with exposed brick and timber-framed walls, thrums with a sinister presence. This blacksmith shop was Pirate Lafitte's cover.[58] Pirates stole goods from ships,[59] murdered or enslaved the survivors and sold the treasure they stole. They got into drunken assaults with each other.[60] Lafitte, the most famous of these pirates, robbed goods from countless ships. He murdered anyone who got in his way. Hid his bloody fortune nearby in the Atchafalaya Basin, the largest river

Lafitte's at Dusk. Photograph by Rachelle O'Brien.

swamp in America. (Follow the advice of our friend, an oil ship captain: don't go there. And if you find yourself traveling on the water at night, don't stop *for any reason*. This Louisiana shipmaster once saw the ghost of his dead wife on the ship there and later spotted the face of a ghost clown in his bathroom mirror. Local seamen dare not come close to the Atchafalaya Basin. They avoid Lafitte and his ghost pirates whenever possible.)

Where does that bad energy come from? It is from death, y'all. It is from theft, fraud, murder. Pirates can slit your throat, stab you in the back for a buck.

We sit at a rough-hewn table near the epic piano where local musicians like Eric Laws strum the keys. But shadows move in the dim light. Dark mists emerge. I (Rosary) excuse myself. I (Rory) order a shot of tequila. Do we really want to meet up with all these ghost pirates who died younger than us, wealthier than us?

They cling to this spot, some having died at the age of twenty-six or younger on one of Lafitte's twenty ships.

We think we hear voices of rough men carousing. But we spin around, and no one is there. We don't want pirate haints to appear. What could they do? Poison us. Choke us. Scare us to death. We are prepared to *duck* if glassware flies off shelves without reason. If a pirate ghost gets angry, he'll throw a glass in our direction. Is it humor or malevolence? *Both.* We refuse to provoke these fiends. Dead ones have nothing to lose.

Cold spots. Strange sounds. Scents of tobacco (but no one is smoking). These signal that Jean Lafitte has arrived. A chill zips up our spines in this darkened room of the piano bar. We turn up a hurricane lamp. Would we be able to distinguish him in the shadows?

We imagine the mysterious spectral figure of Jean Lafitte appearing. A broad-shouldered man with a moustache, a green uniform, an otter skin hat and fitted black high boots appears near the fireplace.

I (Rosary) warn my daughter, "Don't talk to him. Shush."

He singles us out, holds up his mug. He takes a swig of unrefined, dark, high-alcohol rum. He smiles with lingering eyes.

"Mom, is he flirting with us?"

"*Do not* respond."

Lafitte could surprise you, seduce you, strangle you. This Terror of the Gulf may want to destroy you in his haunt of smugglers. Don't let his aristocratic charm confuse you. At any moment, he could pull out a firearm or knife. He would rather live one day as a lion than a thousand years as a sheep.

You *don't* need to *stay* inside.

Get out.

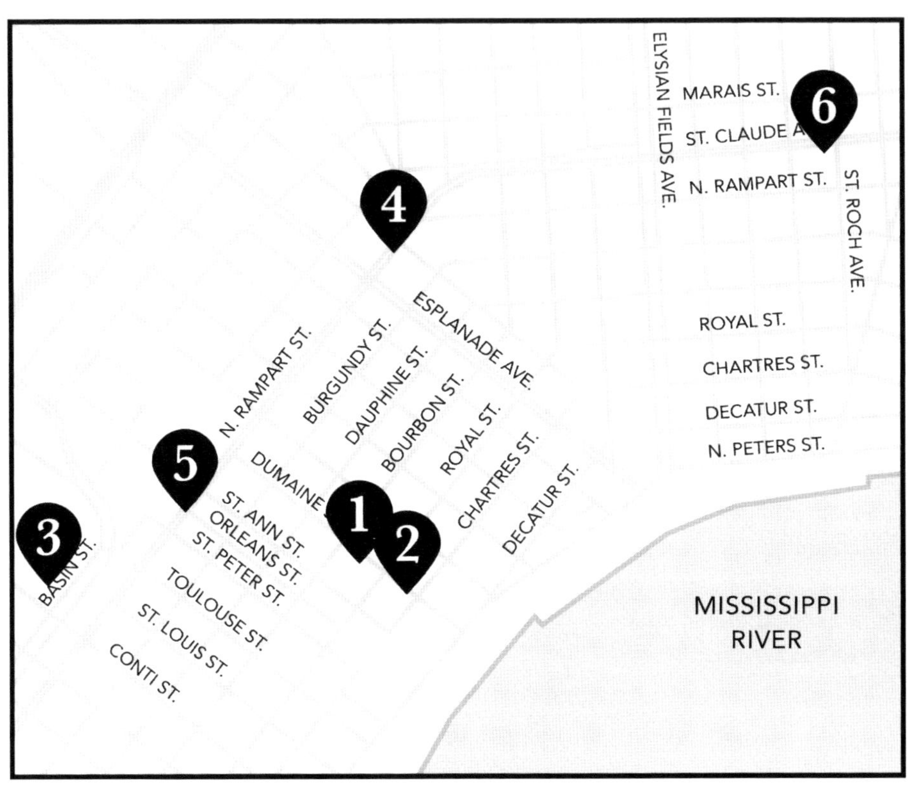

1 Voodoo Museum, 724 Dumaine Street
2 Voodoo Authentica, 612 Dumaine Street
3 Isle of Salvation Botanica, 2372 St. Claude Avenue
International Shrine of Marie Laveau, 2372 St. Claude Avenue
4 Congo Square, 701 North Rampart Street
Louis Armstrong Park, 701 North Rampart Street
5 St. Louis No. 1 Cemetery, Voodoo Spiritual Temple, 1428 North Rampart Street
6 New Orleans Healing Center, 2372 St. Claude Avenue

5

ANCESTOR SPIRITS AND NEW ORLEANS VOODOO

New Orleans is a haunted city, thrumming with so many ghosts that it even scared a Vodou priest from Haiti whom we knew.[61] He didn't like to visit—too many spirits walking underfoot.

Follow us, and you will see how spirits and New Orleans Voodoo are inextricably connected. Skip this chapter if you don't want a fuller understanding of ancestors and the afterlife.

REVELING ANCESTORS AND NEW ORLEANS VOODOO

Friends grip their chairs. Whisper, "What's Voodoo? Is it real?"

Yes, Voodoo is real. Powerful. Evocative. Sacred.

Do you want to heal, know the Divine? New Orleans Voodoo opens the door to the Le Bon Dieu, the benevolent spirit. Connects you with the spirits of your departed ancestors, who protect and guide you.

Our interest in Voodoo since writing *New Orleans Voodoo: A Cultural History* continues to skyrocket. Immersing ourselves in research, we learned that Voodoo practitioners honor God, ancestors and lwas. (Lwas serve as intermediaries for God; they are spirits often syncretized as Catholic saints.)[62] Voodoo is a deep, sophisticated practice that constantly changes, adapts and evolves.[63]

When we die, our spirits live on as ancestors. Voodoo reminds us that larger spirits and ancestors are at always work. These spirits of the dead surround us every day and support us.

Resurrection Garden at St. Mary's Assumption Church. Photograph by Rachelle O'Brien.

Remember the legacy of your ancestors. One priestess[64] told us, "We must always keep their memory alive. We pay homage to them out of love, respect, and gratitude." Another practitioner shared, "Ancestors are in your blood. They are a part of you. However, that relationship needs to be cultivated. It takes work."

Your connection to the spirit world depends on the strength of your connection to your ancestors. You can build this relationship through prayers, altars and rituals. You can feel the ancestors' light and power. Speak their names. Call up their energy and power.

Possession scares people. Does it frighten you? During Voodoo ceremonies, the prayerful invite the possession experience as a way for ancestors to communicate. Are you open to being possessed? I (Rory) am. I (Rosary) am not.

The spirit of an ancestor can enter your body and momentarily take over during a ceremony. (Proper training and preparation are recommended. Possession requires extreme concentration and prayer to get in touch with the Divine.) Being ridden by a spirit can change how you walk, move, talk. You take on different statures, body movements, tones of voice and levels of strength (e.g., an ordinary-sized person can spin a man over their head). Very real and present, ancestor spirits give advice to the living during possession. Isn't there reassurance in knowing the dead are never gone?

STOPPING THE PAIN AND VIOLENCE AT THE VOODOO MUSEUMS: ALTARS TO THE DEAD

You don't have *time* to learn about Voodoo dolls and the Voodoo religion? Why not? Knowledge gained from visiting the Voodoo Museum could embolden you.[65] Respect the dead. Voodoo can help you on your spiritual path. We are all going to die and face the unknown. We, too, will become ancestors. Prayerfully approach the living altars at the Voodoo Museum. Only a fool wouldn't leave an offering. Armor yourself through prayer.

COUNSELING THE BEATEN: READINGS AND TOOLS FOR PROTECTION

Arm yourself with Voodoo tools at spiritual shops, like Voodoo Authentica,[66] the Isle of Salvation Botanica or the Voodoo Spiritual Temple.[67] Purchase gris gris bags, potions, oils and candles.

Schedule a reading with priestesses Brandi Kelley and Miriam Chamani. We've had readings with Haitian-initiated Vodou priestess Sallie Ann Glassman. We watched with reverence as she went into a trance and communicated with spirits. She shared powerful messages with us. If you record the audio of a session, be prepared. Our recording captured the laughter of demons.[68]

Guard yourself against evil spirits. Petition your ancestors to open the pathway for you. Reclaim your power, muscle up, take control of your life on all levels.[69] Follow this priestess's nightly ritual: "Leave an offering on your bedside table. Set up water and a candle. In Voodoo, we say spirits will travel the roadmap of water and light. It's a comfort for any who might be lost or agitated."

Won't these rituals attract bad energy in, you wonder? *No*. You must pay homage to ancestors, saints and the Divine.

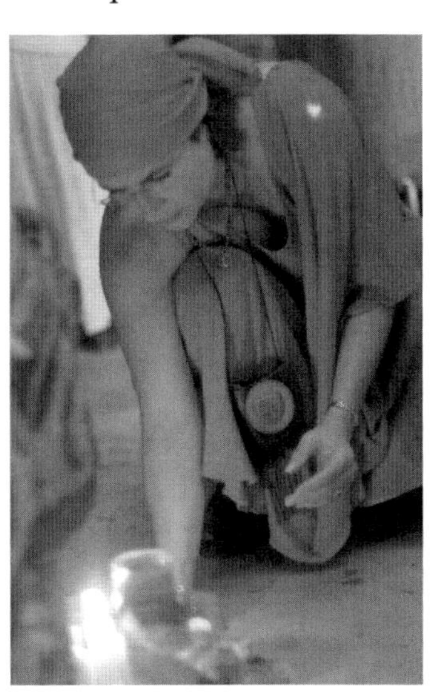

Voodoo Ceremony. Photograph by Cheryl Gerber.

FALLING TO YOUR KNEES AT THE INTERNATIONAL SHRINE OF MARIE LAVEAU

Pay homage to the New Orleans Voodoo Queen, Marie Laveau (1801–1881). Meditate before her mythic sculpture at her international shrine at the New Orleans Healing Center.[70] A brown serpent cloaks her shoulders, provides cosmic protection.[71] Do not fear. No evil one will pop out. Say a prayer at the kneeler. Leave offerings of gratitude, like hair ribbons (Marie was a hair stylist), candles or flowers. The persecutions of the vulnerable persist, whether we want to see them or not.

Door to Marie Laveau's home. *From the Historic New Orleans Collection.*

Who was Marie Laveau? She was a practicing Catholic, a daily communicant, a devotee at St. Louis Cathedral. (Don't stress. You can be a Voodoo and a Catholic. Marie Laveau was.) Voodoo provided a shelter for the broken-hearted and powerless.

Marie Laveau, born in the French Quarter, lived with her chosen partner in an interracial common law marriage on St. Ann Street.[72] She became a powerful leader in the Voodoo community. Marie helped those who suffered from yellow fever with herbal medicine. She comforted the imprisoned, buried the dead.

A Voodoo priestess in New Orleans, told us, "There's more to Marie Laveau than just this big scary witchy archetype. We don't want all her secrets revealed—better to keep some of the magic....There's a reason you feel her. I still feel her in the city for sure." Suddenly, her house lost electricity. It was a sunny day, not a thundercloud in the sky. Indeed, Marie makes herself known.[73]

The spirit of the Voodoo Queen persists. Keep your eyes open for Marie Laveau strolling the city. Some say she never died. She walks the city and St. Louis Cemetery No. 1 at night with her red and white tignon tucked around her head. She flaunts brilliantly colored clothes. As soon as you spot her, she disappears.

Yes, we will seek out more knowledge of the dead. Join us at Carnival and meet the spiritual descendants of Marie Laveau. Mardi Gras Indians wear handcrafted suits that are infused with spirit and are prayerful, like walking altars. If you are lucky, you'll may even spot the Skull and Bones Gang. They'll remind you to "Be good!"

DANCING WITH SNAKES: CONGO SQUARE AND LOUIS ARMSTRONG PARK

Stride under the arch of light that identifies Louis Armstrong Park. Let's pay our tribute to Marie Laveau at Congo Square, the birthplace of jazz. This is the sacred spot where the Marie Laveau led the prayerful on Sundays. She helped the community grieve. She confronted and called on their ghosts. Restored women with a sense of agency.

To overcome grief, Marie Laveau defied it, danced with snakes in Congo Square. Drumming and singing fired up the crowds.[74] She chanted and channeled the ancestors. How did she call upon the dead?

Possession. Spirits would incarnate in her body, possess her, unite with her. The Voodoo Queen was in an ecstatic state for a minute, and then she could communicate with the dead. What messages did she reveal from the other side?

After Marie's death, her daughter, Marie Philomene Glapion, became the leading Voodoo Queen of the city. Both Marie I and Marie II inspired others to fight evil and to reclaim the peace of God.[75]

You may be reading this book because you wake up anxious at night. New Orleans Voodoo can help. There's a saying in New Orleans: "You don't find Voodoo. Voodoo finds you." Well, it found us. Right now, Voodoo is finding *you*.

A NEW ORLEANS GHOST TALE: CLOSING THE VORTEX

I refuse to sleep in the underground, unfinished guest bedroom in my sister's Uptown home, where it feels like spirits zip out of a vortex.

One night, I woke up and saw an ancient ghost staring at me. He was the oldest person I'd ever seen, with deep-set wrinkles carved into his forehead and cheeks. I turned my head the other way and tried to go back to sleep. Then I felt him circle around to the other side of the bed, bend over and watch me. I screamed, "You shouldn't be here!" He vanished.

Weeks later, a mute zombie arrived. A husky ghost stood in a trance next to the bed. His eyes were glazed over, and his arms were raised.

Then children spirits visited. A little boy and girl giggled outside my bedroom. I went back to sleep, and then the boy ghost tugged my ponytail. I hadn't ever been touched by a ghost. Did he just break the rules? An alarmed nurse in Mandeville told me the next day, "He was a demon, not a ghost." I called a Voodoo priestess for counsel and asked her to visit the home to help me remove these spirits immediately from the basement.

VOODOO COUNSEL

Some places (and people) in New Orleans are more haunted than others. They host popular entries for ghosts. Magnetize spirits to remain. Some argue that ghost sightings are imagined, dreamed, hallucinated—not real. What's the truth? We'll know when we're dead.

If you've ever woken up startled because you felt like someone who shouldn't be there was watching you, call on New Orleans Voodoo for help. A friend woke up in the middle of the night and heard two male ghosts carousing. One stopped and said, "Shhh. She can *see* us." She turned on the lights. No one was there. Are there certain people who can see ghosts? Can ghosts tell? Do they care?

For counsel, call on a trusted spiritual advisor. We reach out to Sallie Ann Glassman, a Haitian-initiated Vodou priestess in New Orleans.

What's involved in a spiritual cleansing for a home? Purchase the needed materials: rum, candles, pancake mix, leafy greens, perfume, rubbing alcohol and an egg. (The priestess texted the list to me twice, and they vanished from my cellphone twice. A reminder: spirits can interact with electronics). Trust the priestess.

When I (Rory) met Sallie Ann on the steps of the home, she was dressed all in black, from head to toe. She turned to me, "Tell me about the energy." I responded, "I felt negative energy downstairs. Most of what I've seen has been in the guest bedroom. It feels scary downstairs."

Without blinking, she stated, "Let's go down there."

I led her into the creepy basement. The hair on the back of my neck was standing up. She said, "I feel it right away.'"

I explained, "I used to sleep down here, but I don't anymore."

"It's a good thing you *don't sleep* down here." (What is she seeing that I cannot?)

Taking the risk of sounding nuts, I asked her, "Are there spiritual vortexes where spirits are the strongest?"

"Yes."

The priestess changed into all white clothing. She performed a vortex ritual to clear the spirits. She banged on pots and pans. She made a lot of noise to scare the spirits out. She cleansed the entire house because the spirits were sneaking upstairs to hide. She felt them retreating into the underground storage area, the unfinished part of the basement. She created ritual drawings made of cornmeal, called vèvès (symbolic Vodou drawings) on the ground. Afterward, she took a shower to remove the negative energy and changed into her black clothing. She didn't want spirits to imprint on her.

The priestess explained that the spirits weren't evil or bad. They just didn't understand what tragically happened to them. She felt like it was a *family of ghosts*. She asked them, "Please leave so that another family here could have the time to enjoy the home. Return to the elements. Build up your energy. Reincarnate."

The priestess was calm before and after this exorcism. The basement's energy feels lighter and brighter. But I still will not sleep there.

PROTECTION FROM GHOSTS

Techniques to manage ghostly presences vary widely, from spiritual rituals, like home blessings, to personal communication.

Our recommendation? Protect yourself from the dead.

1. Trust your instincts.

Pay attention to your body, you can sense when things don't feel right. Leave the situation or say a little prayer. One religious friend advised: "When you get more into the spiritual world and more into the good, the bad may also follow." Be prepared for spiritual warfare.[76]

2. Do energy clearings and positive visualizations.

Energy clearings can also help. Our Wiccan friend,[77] who was raised in the United States and in South Africa, recommended:

> *If you are in a negative space, imagine your body being flooded with golden light. Watch the gold light washing the dark energy out of your system. It's visual work, but it also always carries a feeling.*
>
> *You can imagine yourself covered in a blanket of golden light, like a sleeping bag of golden light. You can say powerful positive affirmations, repeating something that is meaningful to you and feels like whatever you believe in. For me, it's "Father, Mother, God, cleanse and purify the space with the white light of love." These visualizations are very powerful because they carry energy that's the opposite of what the negative spirits are.*

A psychic trainer taught us another exercise:

> *Fuel your protective light. Slowly spread your hands apart. Bring them together.*
>
> *When you feel that resistance, that is your white light. You can make it as big as you want, whatever shape you want.*
>
> *Spread it across your body. Fill the whole house with it. Do everything to keep bad energy out.*[78]

3. Use the power of prayer.

Diverse spiritual practices can help. One devout Christian friend told us:

> *Every time you want to remove a ghost, you have to say, "In Jesus's name, you can't be here. You're not welcome here in the presence of Jesus; you can't stay. You must leave in the name of Jesus."*
>
> *Then you have to open a door so the spirit can leave. Negative spirits or demons cannot be in the presence of Jesus. Say it multiple times until you feel like it's left.*[79]

4. Do an energy scan. Tell the ghost, "I don't want to see you."

Energy is around us; spirits float around us. Some are good. Some are bad. No matter, the limp are easily vulnerable to the vicious.

Everything in this world is made up of energy. Feed yourself positively, and your energy is going to be positive. But if you have a lifetime of doing bad things, your vibration becomes negative. That negative energy can persist after death.

Pay attention to energy. Scan the energy of a spirit you encounter. If you feel a ghost has negative energy, immediately shut that down. Be direct. Say, "I'm not interested in seeing you." Spirits can get their power from your reaction. If you are afraid, they will feed on that, become stronger. But they're *not* more powerful than you. You are much more powerful than they will ever be. There's just this strength you must pull up inside of you.

5. Evict the ghost.

Open your door. Open your window. Tell the ghosts they can't be here. Yell if you must. They will find another place to live. If it's a regular ghost (a normal person like you and me), they'll go back to wherever they were. That's the only place they know. They will just take off.

6. Join a supportive community.
Find a trusted friend to share your ghost encounters with. Discuss your theories of the afterlife. Search for ways to cope. Consider joining a support group like OPUS (Organization for Paranormal Understanding and Support), a nonprofit with four thousand open-minded members.

7. Call a professional.
Request help. Maybe it's a paranormal investigator,[80] a friend from church or temple, a priest, priestess, rabbi, monk or nun.

Some holy priests and priestesses shut down spiritual vortexes that are bursting with energy. They create a sacred space and then move the negative spirits into it. They banish evil spirits for good.[81]

Our paranormal investigator friend Charlotte studies EVPs (electronic voice phenomena) in her ghost investigations. She warns that if the spirit is demonic, you need a religious leader to help.[82]

Priests can perform house blessings and cast away darkness. But if there's a demon problem, some New Orleans Episcopal priests call their bishops.[83]

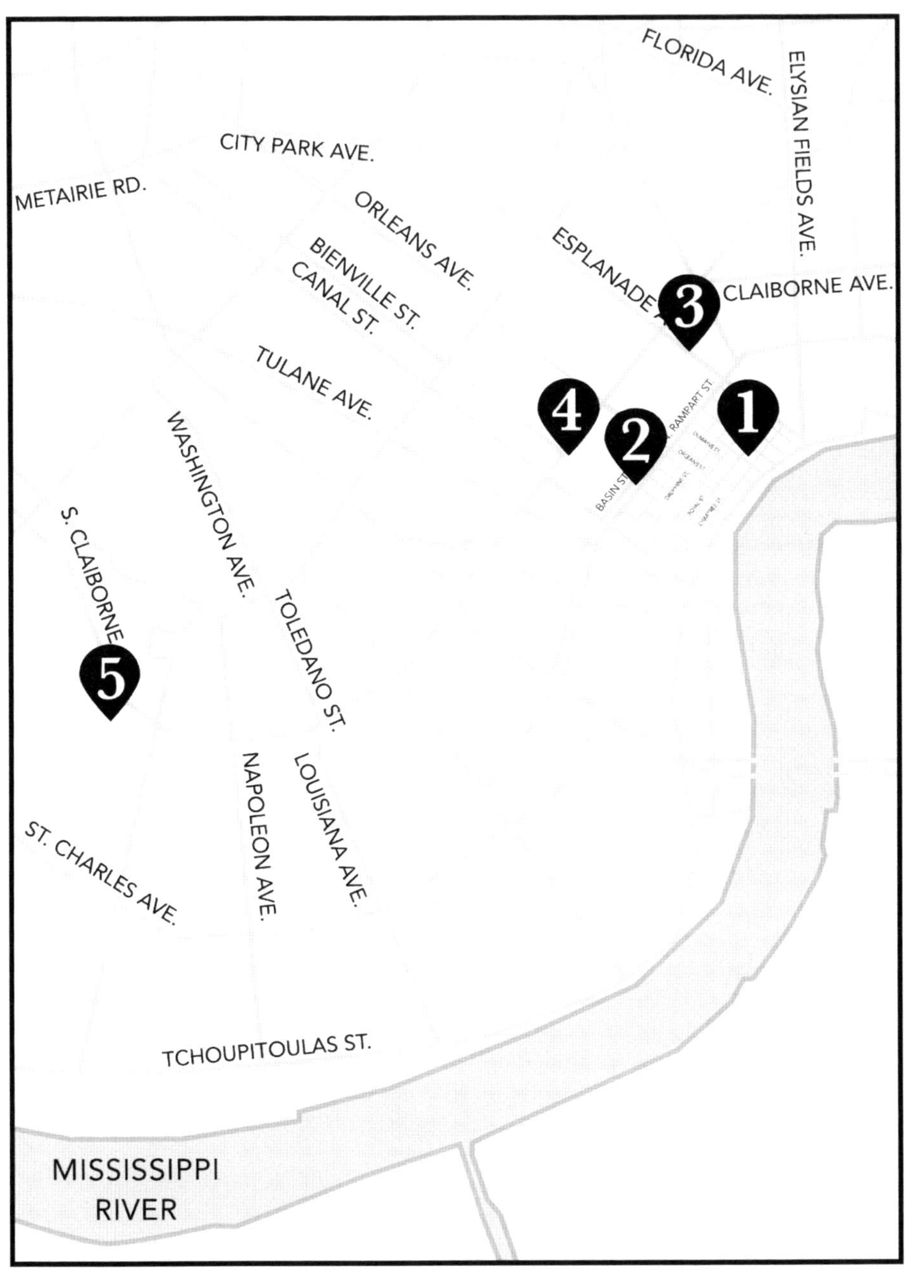

1 Old Ursuline Convent, 1100 Chartres Street
2 Our Lady of Guadalupe Church, 411 North Rampart Street
3 St. Anna's Episcopal Church, 1313 Esplanade Avenue
4 St. Louis Cathedral, St. Louis Cemetery No. 2, 300 North Claiborne Avenue
5 National Shrine of Our Lady of Prompt Succor, 2701 State Street

6

SAINTS AND SINNERS

We don't know about you, but we pray when we're scared, when the room darkens, when we fear what lurks in the shadows. Will an angry dementor hurl us out of bed and slam us against a glass door? Will a lost spirit sit on the side on the bed and *wait for our last breath*? Will the ghost of a wee little girl with woeful eyes take our hands and ask, "Why am I dead?"

We need a spiritual power outside of ourselves in a society that often tells us to exist only for ourselves. Will studying ghosts help us understand what remains for us in the afterlife? What will we be elevated to?

We pray that the spirits of brave holy ones are among the dead presiding over New Orleans. We hope the saintly dead will provide light to combat the darkness, offer protection to diminish the pain.

We admire the brave holy ones whose spirits beckon in New Orleans: Henriette de Lisle, Elizabeth Seton and Martin de Porres. These saints offer hope in the afterlife.

HOLINESS AS A PREVENTATIVE: HENRIETTE DE LISLE AND THE SISTERS OF THE HOLY FAMILY

Henriette de Lisle was born in the year of the Battle of New Orleans (1812), an outcast of sorts, like Pirate Laffite. She had her own battles to fight, born as she was into a brilliant mixed-race family[84] at a time of intense racism, persecution

St. Louis Cathedral, Back. Pen and ink drawing by Billy Harris.

and injustice. Henriette was fueled with a fierce desire to save the enslaved and broken.[85] A huge plaque emblazoned with her name honors Henriette behind St. Anthony's Garden of St. Louis Cathedral. Touch it. Feel her power.

When the Catholic Church barred her from becoming a nun because of her race, Henriette bravely founded the Sisters of the Holy Family. Where did she get her extraordinary courage? How can we learn from her brilliance? What would it take for us to form a band of sympathizers, march toward the scene of decay and slaughter, form an outlaw group of nuns?

Mother Henriette buried the dead in St. Louis Cemetery No. 2 and comforted the desolate they left behind. Join us as we return to that repository at the intersection of Claiborne Avenue and Iberville Street that was created for the overflow of yellow fever victims. When she visited this cemetery, did souls call out to her, "Can you see us?"

Small white crosses blanketed the ground, and desolate mothers and fathers lost their minds, bludgeoned into silence. Some never got over their loss, never got used to it. They woke up sobbing. Grief is greedy like that. Finding a toddler's sock under a footstool can buckle you to your knees.

Gray Day. Photograph by Rachelle O'Brien.

Did the deaths of her own two babies pummel Henriette?[86] Did this fling her to help others to stop up her own bleeding heart? Was she driven to serve rather than sink? To use holiness as a preventative for pain and a prescription for it?

Henriette's spirit strengthened after her death in 1862. Almost a saint (she's currently in the process of being canonized),[87] she performed two miracles through her intercession, healing a four-year-old girl in Texas and a nineteen-year-old woman in Arkansas.[88] Do you believe in miracles? We do.

We approach Henriette's massive aboveground tomb, where she's buried with fellow nuns. Her coping tomb allowed for a soil burial without the hazard of the casket or bodies floating away. Brick, stone and plaster frame large open chambers. Walls stretch three feet above the ground.[89]

We kneel at Henriette's crumbling tombstone, talk to her decaying remains, close our eyes. We feel a sudden breeze on a breezeless day, like a soft touch on our shoulders. Does Henriette's spirit weave through the graves with teary eyes? Spirits appear in old cities, especially to people who believe in them.

Some ghosts are bound to their traumas, not understanding how or why they died. They can't move to the next plane. Perhaps Henriette's ghost remains a disciple of God, comforting the broken-hearted, both the living and the dead.[90]

Incantations of St. Elizabeth Seton and Protection from Death at Childbirth with the Sisters of Charity in New Orleans

New Orleans has its saints, whom the devout pray to when death is certain. When all hope is lost, locals call St. Elizabeth Ann Seton (1774–1821). The weak and dying once watched the Sisters of Charity (founded by St. Elizabeth Seton) sail through Charity Hospital.[91] They cared for patients battling yellow fever, cholera and leprosy,[92] risking martyrdom themselves.

Elizabeth Seton was the first American-born saint to be canonized. The first miracle attributed to her occurred in New Orleans when a nun made a full recovery from pancreatic cancer in the 1930s.[93] (Our grandfather Dr. James Nix served as one of the surgeons who testified to Vatican representatives.)[94] How do you explain miracles? You can't. All you can do is witness them, testify to the holy ones who have levitated the doomed.

Our family still prays to St. Elizabeth Seton. When she was pregnant with a high risk of death, our mother/grandmother Rosary Nix Hartel prayed to St. Elizabeth. (The Mayo Clinic said she and her baby had as much of a chance of surviving as if she had jumped out of an eleven-story building.) Her prayers were answered. Both she and her son, Joseph Seton Hartel, were spared death at childbirth in 1952.

Mother Seton died over two hundred years ago, but her spirit is working miracles in New Orleans, even if you can't see her. Even if there is no statue, no shrine in New Orleans (like in St. Patrick's in New York), you can fall on your knees and call her spirit.

A New Orleans Ghost Tale: The Faceless Monk

I was sleeping, when a monk with no face appeared at the foot of the bed. There was a black hole of empty space where a face should have been.

I was paralyzed. I tried to call out but couldn't.

Finally, I blurted out, "In the Name of Jesus Christ of Nazareth."

I woke up and it disappeared. I was no longer paralyzed. After I cast it away, it never appeared again.

BILOCATION AND ANIMAL COMMUNICATION: ST. MARTIN DE PORRES

The spirit of Saint Martin is everywhere in New Orleans: UNO, Tulane, our uncle's living room (where his adult-sized statue stands at attention).[95] Locals talk so much about Saint Martin,[96] you'd think he just died. We were stunned to find out he lived four hundred years ago in a different country.

This austere friar instantaneously cured the sick in Peru.[97] Martin was so holy, he could communicate with animals,[98] walk through walls, ascend off the earth, even bilocate (live in two places simultaneously).

Many of us are living alone, dying alone, crying alone. One New Orleanian reminded us, "We've had so much *pain* in New Orleans. We are a very spiritual city with lots of ghosts. We keep the light on for the dead. People have a lot of faith; it gives them hope in their grieving."

REAPPEARANCES AT THE OLD URSULINE CONVENT

Let's visit the prayerful in the French Quarter, call out for spiritual protection in the Old Ursuline Convent, an orphanage, a school for girls, an archbishop's residence and a church.[99] What are these indescribable floating orbs of light that keep reappearing? Luminous crystal discs hover like halos.

Is it Our Lady of Prompt Succor? Her spirit protected the convent during the fires of 1788. Back then, the French Quarter was a village of squat wooden

Ursuline Convent. Photograph by Rachelle O'Brien.

houses that attracted fires. Frantic residents climbed wooden staircases into wooden buildings, which were already collapsed and smoldering. They battled raging flames. This fire destroyed 856 of the 1,100 structures that spanned the south-central Vieux Carré from Burgundy Street to Chartres Street.[100]

The fire rushed toward the convent on Chartres Street. What were the Ursuline Sisters to do? Flee in their long-skirts and starched peeked headdresses? Do nothing and burst into flames? No.

They kneeled to a large wooden statue of Mary and Jesus in their chapel.[101] They prayed, beseeched Our Lady of Prompt Succor for protection. The fire consumed 80 percent of the city but left the convent untouched. The National Shrine of Our Lady of Prompt Succor is located at 2701 State Street in New Orleans. There is a chapel with daily mass.

HOLD BACK THE HURRICANE INCANTATIONS: ESPLANADE AVENUE'S OUR LADY OF GUADALUPE CHURCH AND ST. ANNA'S EPISCOPAL CHURCH

We seek out peaceful places in New Orleans to diminish our anguish, havens to counter the hauntings.

Rain pours as we fly down Rampart Street. We won't think about water rushing, wicked winds blowing suddenly, oak trees smashing cars, cutting loved ones in half. Rampart Street soaks up water so fast, it's almost as if there is a ditch down the middle of the street, full of evil ghosts stumbling from adjacent cemeteries, cackling and procuring for hell. Some believe that sudden changes in temperature, electrical activity and atmospheric pressure can encourage spirits to manifest.

We plunge into Our Lady of Guadalupe Church for cover. We won't wait till tomorrow because we could be dead. Horns, saxophones and trumpets salute jazz mass. Music battles the pain, fights back our worry of ghostly manifestations of the long dead praying next to us in the pews.

Who haunts this church? Probably the souls from the eight thousand bodies resting beneath North Rampart, St. Ann, St. Peter and Dauphine Streets.

Our Lady of Guadalupe Church started as a mortuary chapel two hundred years ago, a pass-through for burials and mass graves. It held two hundred funerals a day and more. This death chapel ferried bodies from the French Quarter into the overcrowded cemetery, St. Louis No. 1.

The sheer number of corpses that passed through weighs the place with gravitas. Can't you feel the sorrow?

Unspoken energy reverberates in spaces like this, quietly unnerves priests, reminds us to follow our instincts. Invisible spirits communicate at another level. Sometimes, you *see* ghosts with your other senses. It's a prehistoric cave dwelling instinct. This old church is trembling. Marble angels quiver beneath a massive painting of Our Lady at the altar. We are hungry for spiritual protection. We pray to the statue of St. Expedite for urgent matters, alongside Catholics and Voodoo practitioners.[102]

Oh no. The stained-glass windows on the walls seem to shudder. The figures inside them staring down at us. Are they crying?

We pay homage to St. Jude, the patron saint of hope and impossible causes, alongside locals.

Powerful spirits are at work. God knows how many good people have been spared from disaster in New Orleans.

We move closer to the life-size statue of St. Jude, clothed in bright red,[103] to see if the relic of his arm is still there (it remains intact two thousand

Dead Tree Lying Down. Photograph by Rachelle O'Brien.

Above: *Haunted History Tours. Photograph by Cheryl Gerber.*

Left: *St. Louis Cathedral Holds Court. Photograph by Rachelle O'Brien.*

Left: *Cabildo Corner of Phantoms*. Photograph by Rachelle O'Brien.

Below: *Streetcar in the Rain*. Photograph by Rachelle O'Brien.

Left: Pontalba Dream. Photograph by Rachelle O'Brien.

Below: In Jackson Square, You're Never Alone. Photograph by Rachelle O'Brien.

Left: *Dreaming at Pirates Alley. Photograph by Rachelle O'Brien.*

Below: *Madame LaLaurie's Haunted House. Photograph by Cheryl Gerber.*

Pontalba Building After the Rain. Photograph by Rachelle O'Brien.

Royal Street, New Orleans. Photograph by Sam Blankenship.

HARTSON

Opposite, top: *Aboveground Tombs, St. Louis Cemetery No. 3. Photograph by Rachelle O'Brien.*

Opposite, bottom: *Crosses at Sunset, St. Patrick's Cemetery. Photograph by Rachelle O'Brien.*

Above: *Rain's Coming, St. Louis Cemetery No. 1. Photograph by Rachelle O'Brien.*

Right: The ghost of Pierre, Muriel's Restaurant. *Photograph courtesy of Deanna Duke.*

Left: *Voodoo Fest. Photograph by Cheryl Gerber.*

Below: *Mardi Gras Indian with Skull. Photograph by Sam Blankenship.*

Right: *The International Shrine of Marie Laveau. Photograph by Rory O'Neill Schmitt, PhD.*

Below: *Priestess Miriam Chamani. Photograph by Cheryl Gerber.*

Above: *Snake, Voodoo. Photograph by Cheryl Gerber.*

Left: *Anne Rice's Mansion and Haunted Orphanage. Photograph by Rachelle O'Brien.*

Left: Hexing a Hurricane. Photograph by Cheryl Gerber.

Right: Priestess Sallie Ann Glassman. Photograph by Cheryl Gerber.

St. Louis Cathedral. Photograph by Rory O'Neill Schmitt, PhD.

Left: Drink in Peace, the Columns Hotel. Photograph by Rachelle O'Brien.

Right: Anne Rice's Tomb, Metairie Cemetery. Photograph by Cheryl Gerber.

Pit, 2021. *Oil on wood, painting by Louise Neiland, courtesy of the artist.*

Left: Devil on Royal.
Photograph by Cheryl Gerber.

Below: Funeral, Harold Dejan.
Photograph by Cheryl Gerber.

Large Oak in City Park. Photograph by Robert Schaefer, Jr.

Dueling Oak. *Photograph by Rachelle O'Brien.*

A Window in the Garden District. Photograph by Rory O'Neill Schmitt, PhD.

Big Chief Sunpie and the Northside Skull and Bones Gang. Photograph by Sam Blankenship.

Uncle Lionel's Funeral. Photograph by Cheryl Gerber.

A New Orleans Ghost Tale: Spirit Intercession

A New Orleans taxi driver shared:

I pray to Saint Jude every day, visit his shrine weekly. My family has done so for thirty-five years. I drive a cab that's red in honor of his color, carry his picture, give out holy water. I would be dead now if it wasn't for St. Jude. I was driving along in the French Quarter, and a violent force made my car stop mid-street, shoved my car back. Must've been my guardian angel or Saint Jude who halted the car because a file of little children ran in front of me. I would have killed them if I hadn't stopped. I could never have lived with that.

years later).[104] Focus on the blinking red vigil lights that flank the shrine. The shadows lurking about could be ghosts or Saint Jude protecting us.

God knows how many spirits loiter around. We refuse to stand here, petrified of the ghosts we're seeing, sensing, fearing. We're leaving this church now before we collapse—or become possessed.

We sail over to Saint Anna's Church, sandwiched between flooding Rampart Street and the rising Mississippi River.[105] We need a priest to bless our new rosaries that we picked up at St. Catherine's shrine in Paris.

As we enter the candlelit church, sounds assault us—heavy breathing, incense clicking (priests use so much incense to cover the humidity). Is there some big *evil* coming?

Huddled hopeful ones pray against a hurricane. We blanket ourselves in their support. We can't lean on our own thin knowledge.

Lightning rips the sky. Thunder jolts the prayerful.

We step down the aisle, feel the trembling ground. Is the church sinking? Will the squatted building lift off its foundation? We ignore the gasping wind outside, hunch forward, focus straight ahead. We won't be distracted by the shadows moving in our periphery. The statues staring seem to be quivering, even crying. Is there a statue we could hold onto so we don't get propelled into a

Michael, Lead the Way. Photograph by Rachelle O'Brien.

A New Orleans Ghost Tale: Even the Religious Are Haunted

Two ghosts are always having conversations in the hallway at Christ Church Cathedral on St. Charles Avenue. Staff hear their phantom footsteps stomping down the hallway so frequently, they accept the paranormal as normal.

After I closed up the church one night, my husband and I are alone looking at items in the rummage sale room—the Parish Room has always been an uncomfortable space at the end of the hall. It's getting darker. I feel a negative energy reverberate. It's unnerving, unsettling, feels like we're not *alone. I tell my husband, "I feel like somebody's going to come down that hallway. We need to leave immediately."*

We hear loud bang. It startles us. Sounds like somebody slammed a silverware drawer on the ground. We race out of there. At the front door, I set the five-digit alarm code and leave. Then, I wait outside because any movement inside will set off the alarm. I think for sure there's somebody coming down the hallway. But the alarm doesn't go off.

The next day, I look at the security cameras, thinking there's probably a plausible explanation, like a rat or a mouse knocked something down. I watch the security video. There's nothing in the hallway. No rodent. No person. No ghost. No one was there, nothing to explain the crashing.

hurricane death? If we die in this church, will we join the holy ones on the other side?

We need warrior strength, like the patron saint of New Orleans had. Let's visit Saint Joan of Arc's giant golden statue overlooking Decatur Street. We beseech her to bear her sword and lead us to the divine. Joan, nineteen, said the name of Jesus while being burned at the stake. Joan, unschooled, claimed that Saint Michael, Saint Catherine and Saint Margaret spoke to her through visions. They told her to lead an army to return France to the French.

Can we call on the holy dead for help?

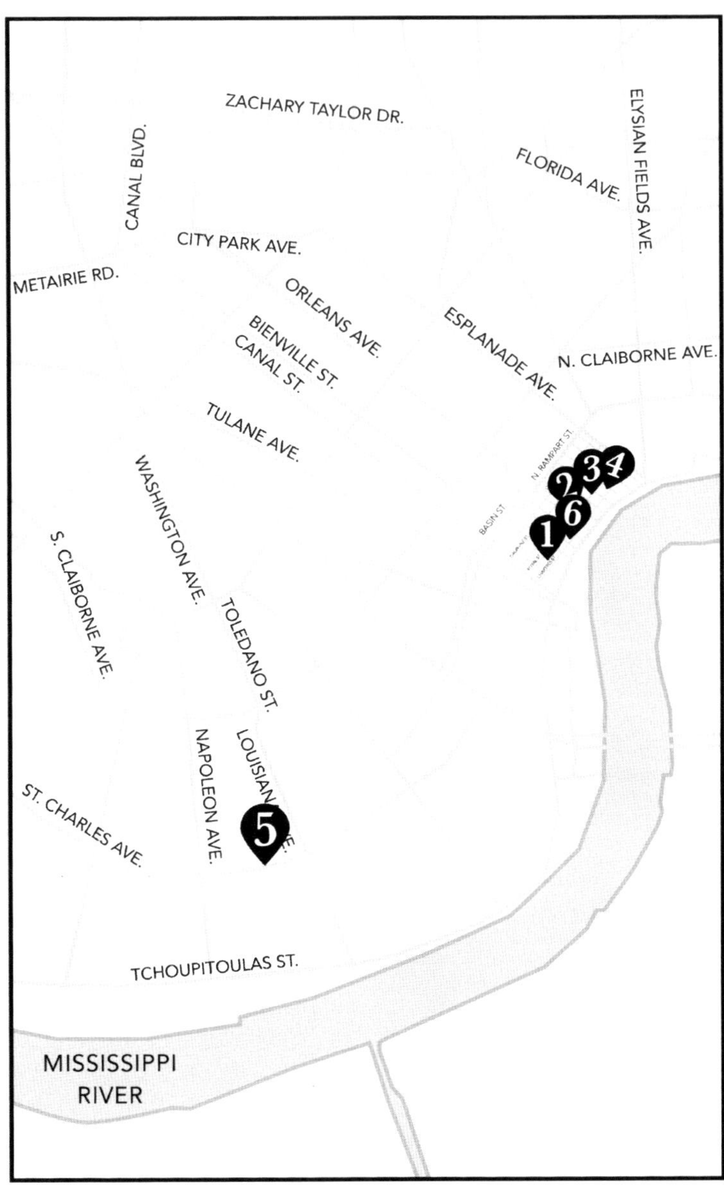

1 Hotel Monteleone, 214 Royal Street
2 Bourbon Orleans Hotel, 717 Orleans Street
3 Andrew Jackson Hotel, 919 Royal Street
4 Hotel Villa Convento, 616 Ursulines Avenue
5 The Columns Hotel, 3811 St. Charles Avenue
6 Omni Royal Hotel, 621 St. Louis Street

7

HAUNTED HOTELS

HAVENS FOR THE DEAD

Ghosts take up residence in New Orleans, haunt oak-lined avenues, loiter in crumbling cemeteries, spend eternity in five-star luxury hotels. Wouldn't you?

Empty rooms feel so full here. Spirits seem to just be hanging around, waiting to make contact. Why do they remain in the Crescent City? Is the veil thin in this part of the world, where the dead and the living can exist side by side?[106] Are spirits prisoners of their own tragedies, confined to buildings that soaked up their pain and replay it?[107]

Let's spoil ourselves at the finest hotels in New Orleans, where your neighbor just might be a ghost.

DEAD GUEST SIGHTINGS AT HOTEL MONTELEONE

We glide past twin doormen, who graciously swing open massive golden doors to the Hotel Monteleone.[108] The host with the most *ghosts*. Be prepared for ghost activity in the French Quarter. Don't say we didn't warn you.

Let's skip up the steps and jump aboard the rotating Carousel Bar, sip a Ramos gin fizz as we feel the pastel-colored world go round and round and wait for the hauntings to begin.

Pause a second. Breathe deep. The twinkling yellow lights at the Carousel Bar are flashing on and off. Is that typical? No. Who or what is doing that? We're uncertain.

Above: Hotel Monteleone. *Photograph by Rachelle O'Brien.*

Left: *Round and Round We Go. Photograph by Rachelle O'Brien.*

Oh *no*! Did a figure in period clothing just vanish? Was it a ghost or just a steampunk running late to catch his flight?

We've heard the rumors that guests hear voices in empty rooms, see shadowy figures out the corners of their eyes. Guests report waking up in the dead of night, only to see a shadow sitting on their bed. We are committed to our research, but do we dare sleep here? *We dare.*

We squint into the big mirror, search for faces of individuals absent in the room. We look over to the grandfather clock. Nope. We don't see any ghostly faces. Yes, his eyes will expand and gloat at you if…try not to think about it. Instead, we sip a sazerac and just linger on this high stool. Gaze at Royal Street, where some dress as devils for fun.

We wipe the sweat from our brows, get up slowly, one step before the other. We head toward the restaurant for a chicory coffee. We act like everything is normal when we introduce ourselves as ghost authors to the hostess. Will she label us as freaks, mystics, ghost hunters? Unwell, unhinged, unwanted?

An immediate knowingness radiates from her eyes. *Yes.* She smiles and says, "They're *everywhere.*" *They*? *Everywhere*?

I (Rory) tell the hostess, "I woke up last night around 2:00 a.m. I felt like someone was in my hotel room, watching me. But no one was there."

"*Yep.* It's probably Maurice. He can go anywhere. He goes everywhere. He especially likes to play with the housekeeping staff—ruffle up fresh beds, shut recently opened blinds, steal night chocolates from their carts." She turns on twinkle toes and leads us to the back of the restaurant.

Maurice? His name is mentioned casually, just like the living. They've accepted this specter as fact.

We are hungry for more, but she drops the conversation, goes silent. There's likely a staff onboarding rule that dictates an allowable amount of ghost talk. And we have hit our limit. She guides us to take our seats by giant windows overlooking Royal Street. She points to the linen selection. We choose the white (not the black) linens to match our skirts.

The maître d'hôtel approaches and tells us, "I'm OK with ghosts, as long as they don't mess with my paycheck." He chuckles as he shares his ghost encounters, as if laughing will reduce some of the terror. (It doesn't.)

Will a chair fly from the table on its own? Will a garbage bag suddenly open up and flap about as if a spirit is rifling through it? (We saw his video.) Will we hear voices chatting in the *empty* back office? Will a ghost hand *grab* our shoulders, pull us back from the food prepping station, too?

We are here to investigate Monteleone's legends (and to revive ourselves with andouille gumbo and Creole crab cakes). We wait to see if the ghost chef and waiter will feud over door politics. Will we catch a phantom employee, like Red Wildemere, lurking about? Between sips of bloody Mary, we dart our eyes to check for a fierce-looking man with dark hair, the original Monteleone owner. This ghost never stays long enough for a deep look.

After lunch, we gaze past a display cabinet of antique books. Famous dead authors, Monteleone guests, may be dropping in soon: Anne Rice, Tennessee Wiliams, Ernest Hemingway, William Faulkner, Truman Capote.[109] Could they give us a quote for our book? We push our blond hair behind our ears, slap on bloodred lipstick and saunter into the glamorous lobby. This hotel has been providing luxurious accommodations since 1886. You think if we loiter, we'll see a dead literary celebrity? We might.

We need to keep *moving*. We head upstairs to our plush room in the Iberville tower, where king cake and champagne await. Oh *no*! We swallow hard. Invisible footsteps follow those who dare to enter the empty hallways.

We step into an unexplainable freezing spot. Wait. Did someone just brush past us? We don't dare turn around. No one's there, and that's normal here.

Room 419. We pass the threshold into our room. Shut the door *quick*!

There may be something to people having died in these *hotel rooms*. Guests wake up and hear dense breathing, and it feels like something is floating past them. They get up, walk about and feel a presence of someone looking at them. But they don't see anything. (Indeed, we experienced something similar.) Thank God, unseen hands didn't poke at us while we tried to rest.

What happened to those who died here? Restless cholera victims, who clung to bed posts and vomited and then collapsed? Why do their spirits return? Did they choose to leave their tombs to briefly recall this flicker of joy, this flicker of love, this flicker of life at the Hotel Monteleone?

Is nobody at the hotel in charge of getting rid of the undead?

We met an excited and alarmed hotel guest after she'd a ghost encounter. She introduced herself as a biologist, likely to gain credibility (we understand). She was riding the elevator alone, heading down from the fourteenth floor. Suddenly, the button to the fourth floor illuminated. It had been pushed. By whom? She held up her hand to about three feet high and pointed out that this button was at just about the height of a child. She said it was *Maurice*.

We need strength to deal with child ghosts. Maurice? Was he French?

Prepare yourself for a devastating story.

In the 1800s, Jacques and Josephine Bergere wanted to feel inspired by creativity, to experience the strong emotions at the French Opera House

Ghost Boy, the Monteleone Hotel. *Photograph courtesy of Deanna Duke.*

just a few blocks away from Hotel Monteleone. They went out for a night on Bourbon and Toulouse Streets. The couple never dreamed it would be dangerous to leave their little boy with the nanny in room 930. Who imagined they would come home to a child dead from a high fever, a God-knows-what bacterial infection? Scarlet fever? Cholera? Illness slayed Maurice Bergere almost instantly.

The mother, in a state of shock, needed to connect with her son again. She prayed nonstop and even held séances. Did her husband feel she was delusional or crazed? His wife wanted to see her boy one more time. If she didn't, maybe she would self-destruct, thrust her feelings into the world of regret and never come out again.

Josephine returned to that explicit scene of his death in room 930. She knew for certain his shadow lingered. Her soul ached for him. She would find a way to reach her boy. She called, and he answered. Early one morning, little Maurice appeared at the foot of her bed, saying, "Mommy, don't cry. I'm fine." He sprang to his mother. He wanted to put back together the broken puzzle of her shattered heart.

Maurice's ghost walks in and out of guest rooms at night. Is he searching for his parents? Others insist he stalls the elevator on the fourteenth floor. (It's not really the fourteenth floor. It's actually the thirteenth floor, but they skip the number thirteen in the naming of the floors.) Sometimes, he throws objects, pushes tables, hides items. He makes books fly off the shelf by themselves, creates a mess, causes a ruckus—entertainment for the dead.

Maurice and other mischievous ghost children race down hallways, playing tag. They giggle in closets. Some guests see these ghost children materialize wearing gloves to cover their fingerless hands. When they look at their pallid faces, they vanish.

We listen for the rattling in the attic. Ghost children playing hide-and-seek in the afterlife.

A NEW ORLEANS GHOST TALE: EVICTING A DEMON

I was trying to help remove a ghost from a troubled hotel with my paranormal investigation team. But soon, I learned it was a low-level demon. It ripped the heavy air conditioner off the wall. Hurled it across two rooms.

Members of my team rushed in to help me. But the demon grabbed one woman's cross on her neck. Lifted it straight up. Seized one guy's privates. Squashed my cheeks bloody.

The demon screamed like a rageful creature: "Get out!"

We left. But this demon followed me home. *Suddenly, my arms were being scratched.*

You see, a normal ghost will just take off. But others, you must mentally and physically throw them out. Tell them they can't be here. I opened the door, kicked the demon out of my car.

WAYWARD SINNERS OF THE BOURBON ORLEANS HOTEL

Get these ghosts out of our heads. Get us off our feet. Get us to Bourbon Street.

Bourbon Street imbues a unique personality—joy, tinged with sorrow, despair mixed with wild outrageous laughter, a strange kind of hope. Bourbon attracts the curious, a path to fantasy and wild fun. But past tragedies linger in ghostly activity in the French Quarter. All the fires, hurricanes and epidemics create an uneasy feeling, like death's around the corner.

Spend time in the French Quarter, and you'll experience a haunting eventually. Our friend, who's a French Quarter resident, shared, "Late last night, I felt cold fingers on my neck. I turned around, but there was nothing there. Sometimes, shadows pass down my hallway, as if somebody is walking under the lights. I peak my head out of my bedroom to look out. But no one is there."

Invisible ghosts creep—but no matter! We need to keep *going*. We jaunt to the Bourbon O Bar and order Grandma's favorite, an old fashioned. (When we were kids, she taught us to make hers with bourbon, two packets

A Day on Chartres. Photograph by Rory O'Neill Schmitt, PhD.

of Sweet 'N Low and Coke at her home on Fontainebleau Drive.) Slurp, sip, burp. Onward for the ghost hunt!

We meander into the Bourbon Orleans Hotel, right smack in the center of New Orleans, crouched between the Saint Louis Cathedral and Bourbon Street. We climb onto one of the expansive balconies overlooking the sea of the French Quarter. We're here to meet one of the twenty ghost residents.

"Mom, who would you like to see first—the dancer, soldier, orphan, or—"

"The Suicide Nun!"

Read *no further* if you intend to sleep downtown at the Bourbon Orleans.

Blood-tingling cries of the Suicide Nun ring through the air. Do we need to spend the night in room 646 to get more information? Oh no. Tortured wailing terrorizes guests. Listen for the nun's labored cries. Visitors hobble downstairs in the middle of the night, clutching their robes, fearful of what causes these howls. Shadows creep across the walls. Guests sleep with the lights on because her violent silhouette darkens the chamber. It's like staring into pitch black, devoid of color, light. Suddenly, a figure wearing a nun's habit looms over the bed with a watchful gaze.[110]

A Sister of the Holy Family died by suicide in this room. Was she overcome with grief, having buried too many wild-eyed stricken orphan girls? What shame was she hiding? Did she want to abscond from the nunnery, dance half-naked in a hallway? Leave her life of cloistered isolation? Make love with a wounded soldier?

Does she know the soldier who haunts the sixth floor is looking for her?

This soldier, also known as The Man, limps down hallways. The sounds of his hollow and uneven footsteps linger in the dead of night. Guests hear the scraping of his sword against the flooring and his *groans*. His uniform is always tattered, bloody, as though he has already swallowed the horrors of battle. Is he one of the wounded who was transported to hospitals and convents?[111] Was he cared for by one of the nuns from Henriette's Sisters of the Holy Family? With gaping, violent wounds, he reaches out for help. While the unknown soldier yearns to find someone, we don't know who.

Wait. There's more to be found in this haunted haven. In other rooms, dying orphan ghosts materialize, orphan girls that Sister Henriette De Lille's order cared for. Apparitions of young girls lie in beds with black mists seemingly hovering over them. Feet *pitter-patter* up and down empty halls. A child rolls a ball and chases it down the sixth-floor corridors. Pint-sized spirits tug on patrons' shirttails and bump into their tables, knocking over glasses. Do you hear their laughter?

Up the winding staircase, we venture into the ballroom, known for notorious quadroon balls in the 1800s.[112] A shameful part of New Orleans's history was the *plaçage* system, in which young women of color were partnered with wealthy white men as secret second wives.[113] Some men bought their second families shotgun houses (front to back skinny house with no halls) in the Marigny District on the other side of Esplanade Avenue. Some paid for their children's education abroad.

Under the crystal chandeliers and forty-foot ceiling, gorgeous women once billowed about, wearing décolletés, adorned with silks, satins and gleaming jewels. Will we spot the ghost dancer waltzing with her invisible partner? Her gown's hem dusts the carpeted floor. Here, a bloodstain appears regularly. Is she reliving a quadroon ball, one that Henriette de Lisle famously halted here? Henriette transformed the ballroom into a chapel, nailed a sign over the door that read: "Silence, My Soul; God is Here."

BEIGNET BREAK

While exhuming ghosts, unpacking suspicious specters, we need to take care of our own souls. We make a short detour to the Café du Monde. It's time to drip dusty sugar all over ourselves, make sense of what we are learning, sensing, seeing, fearing.

We kill our gloom by reminding ourselves of Louisiana's legendary heroes, like Marie Laveau, the Baroness of Pontalba, Kate Chopin or Edgar Degas. They strolled these same French Quarter streets, toasted champagne at Mardi Gras soirées, envisioned a future beyond the confines of a stifling society, broke through the walls of betrayal and became victorious.

Reinvigorated with sugar and caffeine, we continue our walkabout to Royal Street. We stroll past the famous nineteenth-century judge's home with its wrought-iron cornstalk fence and prepare ourselves to be the victims of mischief and foolery at the Andrew Jackson Hotel.

HUSKS OF MEN REAPPEARING AT THE ANDREW JACKSON HOTEL

Years before the Andrew Jackson Hotel was built, this site once housed a tragic orphanage and boardinghouse.[114] It harbored the forgotten boys of New Orleans.

We imagine gleeful boys singing "Holy God, We Praise Thy Name," a traditional Catholic hymn of the 1790s, with their families at St. Louis Cathedral on a Sunday, just to be left bereft and alone on the street the next day—motherless, fatherless, futureless.

They became orphans, swarming the French Quarter in the 1790s. Yellow fever had shot through the city and collapsed their families. Raging fires scorched the Quarter, burning more families to death.

Did these forgotten boys turn mean and vile? Defy authority? Become hoodlums set out to punish? Use knives, ice picks, stones, razors, bones? Did they kick through doors? Punch fists through walls? Bite, kick, run?

How long could the Spanish government stomach young hoodlums acting recklessly, defacing property, provoking others, selling stolen goods, stealing, vomiting and defecating in the street? (Left alone, did these boys privately sob for their lost mothers, fathers, sisters, brothers?)

St. Louis Cathedral Glows. Photograph by Rachelle O'Brien.

The Spanish government harbored these orphan boys (aged four to thirteen) in New Orleans.[115] Unprotected boys could get their throats slit for their shoes or jackets. Weren't they lucky to be caught and incarcerated in an orphanage? Tough caretakers tried to tame the sullen, grief-stricken boys, silence their rage through brute force. They forced them into uniforms, shaved their heads, made them walk in regimental lines, quieted them with one crack of a ruler.

Some say the caretakers were controlling and punitive. Did cruelty inspire camaraderie among the little boys? These children just needed a friendly hand, someone to help them stand up because their legs were giving out. They needed someone to heat their food because they had no strength. Someone to nod with compassion because they were extremely sick. They couldn't care for their own basic needs. Did they sob in agony?

The orphanage burned down mysteriously in 1792, killing five boys. Their husks reappear on Royal Street, where their boardinghouse once stood. Why do they keep coming back after their abrupt deaths?

Do the boys even know they died in the fire? Their souls appear caught in the sinister in-between, hiding from adults, still fearful, begging to be saved from the fire—or something worse.

These Walls Have Eyes, Andrew Jackson Hotel. Photograph by Rachelle O'Brien.

Are these vengeful ghosts bent on retaliation? Bringing hell back to the place that abused them, their childhood prison?

We don't want to hear their ghostly cackles polluting the halls, resounding in the courtyard. We don't want to watch objects fly across the room, be the target of their pranks,[116] have our garments disappear, be slapped awake, see our wooden crosses snapped in half, have our blankets yanked off, feel their decaying hands running over our bodies.

But the most active ghosts are those of the young boys. We don't want to play hide-and-seek in the back house with the ghost of Thomas. And when eight-year-old Armond tries to lure us out the window, we are checking out. *Immediately.*[117]

He's a known fiend. During his lifetime, Armond was thrown from the second-floor balcony (or jumped on his own accord). We don't need to hear a psychic medium converse with this boy to believe him when he says, "We are hiding."[118]

Other ghosts abound, like the widow caretaker Sara, who obsessively straightens rooms, plumps pillows, shoves back furniture.[119] Some say the ghost of General Andrew Jackson also haunts this building. Phantom footsteps echo as a full-bodied general in antebellum clothing, a blue wool uniform coat with gold-colored buttons and epaulettes, patrols the second floor.[120] After the orphanage burned down, a U.S. federal courthouse was built on this land. Here, General Jackson was once held in contempt of court. Does his vengeful ghost return to unravel the mystery of the fire and the murders? Is he trying to halt the confusion once and for all?

Are we brave enough to continue? *No.* Will we march onward anyway? *Yes.*

RUNNING AWAY FROM MADNESS AT THE HOTEL VILLA CONVENTO

Be careful in the French Quarter, where evil (both the living and the dead) get violently vicious. Stab you to death. A Catholic priest we knew in New Orleans was murdered like that. He ran a seafarers' home in the French Quarter, feeding, sheltering and caring for seamen. After twenty years of faithful service, he took in a sailor one night who slit his throat.

Next, we'll head to Hotel Villa Convento, once a brothel on a holy street of nuns.[121] This haunted building is rumored to be the House of the Rising Sun.[122] A musician[123] lived in one of the boarding rooms and exposed this destination for what it was. Everyone's familiar with his dreadful lament for a house in ruins:

> *There is a house in New Orleans*
> *They call The Rising Sun*
> *And it's been the ruin of many a poor boy*
> *And God, I know I'm one.*[124]

A NEW ORLEANS GHOST TALE: DEAD PLUMMETING ON BOURBON STREET

Sun Goes Down on Bourbon Street. Photograph by Rachelle O'Brien.

Zach and Addie lived together in the French Quarter, and they rode out Hurricane Katrina together. Zach had been a veteran, and he was in desperate need of mental healthcare, but he didn't get it. He and Addie had a very tumultuous relationship, and they became involved in drug use.

In October 2006, Zach went a block east of Bourbon Street to the Omni Royal Hotel. He sat there for some time and ordered drinks at the bar. Then he went up to the roof and jumped off. He fell five stories and died. His body landed on the parking deck next to the hotel.

Paramedics discovered a set of keys and a disturbing five-page note in his pocket.

Zach wrote: "This was not an accident. My name is Zach. I've taken my own life for the life that I took. Take the keys that are in this bag. Go to my apartment on North Rampart Street, and that's where you'll find the body of my girlfriend, Addie."

The police went there, but they didn't expect to find what they found in the kitchen. Addie's head was in a pot on the stove. Her hands and feet were in another pot. Her arms and legs were in a basing pan in the oven, and her torso was wrapped in saran wrap in the refrigerator. There was blood in the bathtub, along with the saw that he used to dismember her.

Zach and Addie had gotten into a fight, and then he strangled her. A few days later, he decided the best plan to try to get away with this was to cook the soft tissue off Addie's bones and then throw the bones out—like she was an animal. But he found out that this was not as easy as he thought. Guilt set in, and he killed himself.

*Frequently, witnesses state that they see Zach's spirit falling off the side of the Omni Royal Hotel. (This residual haunting occurs so much that, after a while, the police have stopped taking calls about it.) The ghost appears like a shadow and falls right where Zach did—over and over again.**

* A local paranormal historian recounted the life and death of Zach and Addie in New Orleans. Interview with Deanna X, American Ghost Walks guide, New Orleans, September 10, 2024.

Once you enter, you may confront maniac ghosts who arrived by land or sea. Angry ghosts infest the twenty-five rooms there. We don't want you to see residents of ill repute: syphilitic people, gamblers with knives in their backs, victims of suicides in blood-filled tubs, addicts vomiting in rancid urinals, criminals struggling alone for one more breath, their decaying bodies left alone to rot.

Phantoms thrive inside this big, vitriolic hotel. Do you have the guts to face the ghosts of all those gamblers, sailors, sex workers? People with no family, no friends to care for them when they collapsed with typhoid, yellow fever, syphilis—or were murdered in their sheets?

Listen for disembodied footsteps, unexplained music. Look out for lights that flicker, objects that relocate. Your belongings may be yanked from your hands, hurled across the room and then disappear. Please ignore any growling noises.[125] Do you want your hair pulled out? Your body shoved about? We don't either.

If you must stay here, request room 302. The nine-year-old girl ghost wearing a white slip in this room is less threatening.

Be sure you don't get room 209, the suicide room. Ignore the ghost's things if you find them: wallet, pens, coins, tattered linens, remnants of a never-returned-to-life. A strong presence may envelope you when you enter the bathroom. This resident killed himself by slicing his veins with a glass shampoo bottle. You may feel a spirit's heavy grief and anxiety. You may see shampoo bottles unexplainedly plunge from the once bloodstained tub to the floor. Some couldn't shake off the pain and humiliation of being diseased and broke. They pulled the insides of their pockets out to find nothing. We suffer when we think about the forever hopeless. Is it wrong to have empathy for ghosts?

Careful, now. Weird, sexual perversions occur. The Ghost Madame may accost you. Shrouded in black, she peeks out the window, her eyes peeled for strangers. The silent Shadow Man appears with her, stone-faced in complete denial or delight. She calls out your name from the window. "Come on in!" Say, "Hey, baby. Where are you going?"

Was a brothel the only business the Ghost Madame could have had in the late 1860s? These women, with legs spread wide, their starving babes hidden in closets, hands over their mouths, were paid so little. They closed their eyes, licked whatever unbearable thing an angry, sad, deranged customer wanted. Some questioned: How far should I go? They knew vicious customers could terrorize. Strangle them to death. Male clients—though pleasant enough in public—might explode with rage, hatred, perversion in private. Out of the blue, they could punch, stab or choke a woman to death—if they didn't cooperate (and even if they did).

If you decide to visit here, be prepared: invisibles may ride with you in the elevator to the third floor.[126] Listen for chaotic noise, laughter and the sounds of pleasure, rattling from room 301. Brace yourself if you encounter two ghosts making love in this room. Watch them if you must, but freeze. If you hear a knock on the door, do nothing. That's the Ghost Madame signaling the end of a client's time.

Shower quickly. Sometimes, the Madame watches from the doorway.

Do not get intimate in the guestrooms here. The Ghost Madame enjoys watching.

In the middle of the night, the bed may dip as though the Madame has settled next to you. Sometimes, she interacts with men in bed, speaks suggestively to them while they are asleep, strokes their cheeks. When they roll over, they'll wake up to Madame's scary, ominous eyes staring at them.

We leave Hotel Villa Convento. Hum the eerie, sad melody for this house in ruins, once living on evil:

Oh Mother, tell your children,
Not to do what I have done.
Spend your lives in sin and misery,
In the House of the Rising Sun.

THE ELEGANT DEAD REAPPEAR AT THE COLUMNS HOTEL

Time for a change of scenery, a visit into the exquisite Garden District, where the upper crust of wealthy society lives, plays, dies, haunts.

Zip with us on a streetcar as we head down Saint Charles Avenue, windows down, hair flying, bells clanging. Epic white columns glare at us.

We yank the cord above to stop. We exit through the heavy back doors and hop onto the neutral ground. Under the shade of ancient oak trees, the Columns Hotel lures us up the brick path to the front gallery.[127]

It's time to pivot from sadness to the sublime. Treat ourselves to crème brûlée, a rich custard with a caramelized sugar topping.

Have we forgotten the danger? We want to get out of doing this visit. We don't want to show you the massive columns, the massive gallery, massive stairs. God forbid you might hear the eerie sounds of undead talkers.

Columns Hotel. Pen and ink drawing by Billy Harris.

Confront their ghosts—the angry rich, who were mean, vengeful, destructive.

We forge through the gallery, where shadowy creatures slurp down oysters or kick back sazeracs. We can't face the forlorn invisibles inside the moonlit parties, inch past tarot card readers, models swaying by tables, dead violinists slumped in chairs.

We push through the doors into the twenty-foot-wide hallway. Meander past a boy from the Jesuit high school and a girl from the Dominican high school seated at a baby grand piano. It's her eighteenth birthday and they are singing the blues. Did that really happen? Yes. Are they still alive? Here? Older, wiser?

The light is dim. It's hard to see who's real and who's a ghost. Some ghosts look so real, so 4-D that you'd mistake them for the living.

We forge past the expansive two-armed parlors, so big that the right one became famous for its mahogany bar. Let's sip a Columns martini, inhale the glamorous ambiance. Movies, like *Pretty Baby*,[128] have been filmed here.

But freezing spots send shivers down our spines.

We begin to anticipate ghosts. Maybe they're inside the ponderous drapes. Will they shimmy across the floor like roaches? Flatten themselves inside crevices? Slither out a crack in the ceiling, a slit in the fireplace, a loose handle of that chandelier?

We pump martinis into our veins and pray. But dry vermouth, pickled vegetables and a Hail Mary can't stop the otherworldly thrumming.

We distract ourselves, imagine dazzling patrons sashaying through doors, spiraling up the staircase, sighing inside canopied four-poster beds. Some never wanted to leave (so their spirits never did). They preferred to eternally gaze out old-fashioned windows, watch the big oak trees and the barely blue sky forty feet up.

It's not the gloomy ghosts who frighten us; it's the elegant ones. They want us. They want everything about us. To feel, smell, touch. They want to run their fingers over things—soft things, hard things. But they're trapped in invisible bodies. Their energy is running out, as they use all their strength to voice some secret.

Some guests have seen elderly women spirits chatting in the Columns bathroom. No one can make out what they say. What do chic ghosts have to gossip about anyways? The newly arrived sophisticated dead? Scrunchies in fashion again? An illicit affair?

We wait for an impeccably dressed gentleman ghost to materialize and vanish. Guests report hearing his eerie whispers in the Victorian lounge. Is he the previous owner, Simon Hersheim, so proud of his home that he simply must share its wonders with whoever enters?[129]

Will we meet the shuffling child? A strange little girl ghost who wanders on the third-floor balcony. Is she talking outside with her reflection or a little friend? Is she a victim of yellow fever or a tragic accident?

We dare not sleep here, lest we confront unwelcomed visitors. Guests report they awaken in the dead of night to see two doleful women sitting on the bed beside them. Their presence startles. Are these ghosts the house owner's wife and sister? Shortly after moving into this house, they died. *Unspecified* causes. Soon after, Simon swallowed potassium cyanide and joined them. Did both pass away in their bedrooms, striken creatures that they were? Did someone break down the door to get their bodies out? Who closed their eyelids, pulled the sheets over their heads, carried out their lifeless bodies?

We can't wait any longer for terror to strike. Our stomachs growl—then snarl. We must obey. We slink our way to the restaurant, past the sweeping mahogany staircase. Light flickers through the domed stained-glass window like angels' wings.

Do we hear humming? That must be the beautiful ghost, the Lady in White. We want to sing with her, pretend she's not dead. We want to make believe there's a chance to save her life, that she can reach somebody—anybody—again.

Left: The Columns Halls. Photograph by Rachelle O'Brien.

Opposite: Like Sisters. Photograph by Rory O'Neill Schmitt, PhD.

Is the humming coming from the ballroom? We long to see the beautiful ghost floating across the dance floor in her long white dress. Even in death, she slow dances into the night, gazes at the moonlight through the oak trees. She listens to the Saint Charles trolley clacking down the avenue every ten minutes. She watches the streetcar ripple by with the same joy, the same pace, the same slow rhythm, just like when she rode it in her youth.

Dare we follow her as she climbs the grand staircase that winds all the way up (the smooth wood circles to the ceiling)? Who wouldn't want to invite the gorgeousness of her on those velvet stairs to room 10, mint julep in hand?

Maybe she'll revel in the privacy of her bedroom under the high ceilings, take comfort in living in this mansion forever. Maybe she'll stand before the mirror of the marble-topped dresser and brush her hair for one hundred strokes? Careful, now. Our Irish grandmother chided: vanity is a sin. The devil will come for you.

Does this ghost wash her hands in an exquisite china bowl with a pitcher, just an arm's reach from the bed? Does she melt into the thickly pillowed bed, scissor her long legs around the quilted chenille bedspread, spread open the

floor-to-ceiling woven wool curtains, pull up the tall windows to invite in the thick, wet, Louisiana night? Does she fantasize as she awaits her shadow lover?

Knock. Knock. The Gentleman Ghost has been spotted at the door to room 10. When this well-dressed specter enters her room, will he embrace her, suckle her breasts, lift her as he flies her to the luscious king-sized bed? Will they delight in each other throughout the night?

Ghost erotica—not what we had planned for. But alas, it's the product of phantom musing. Ghosts can participate in activities they did when they were living, after all.

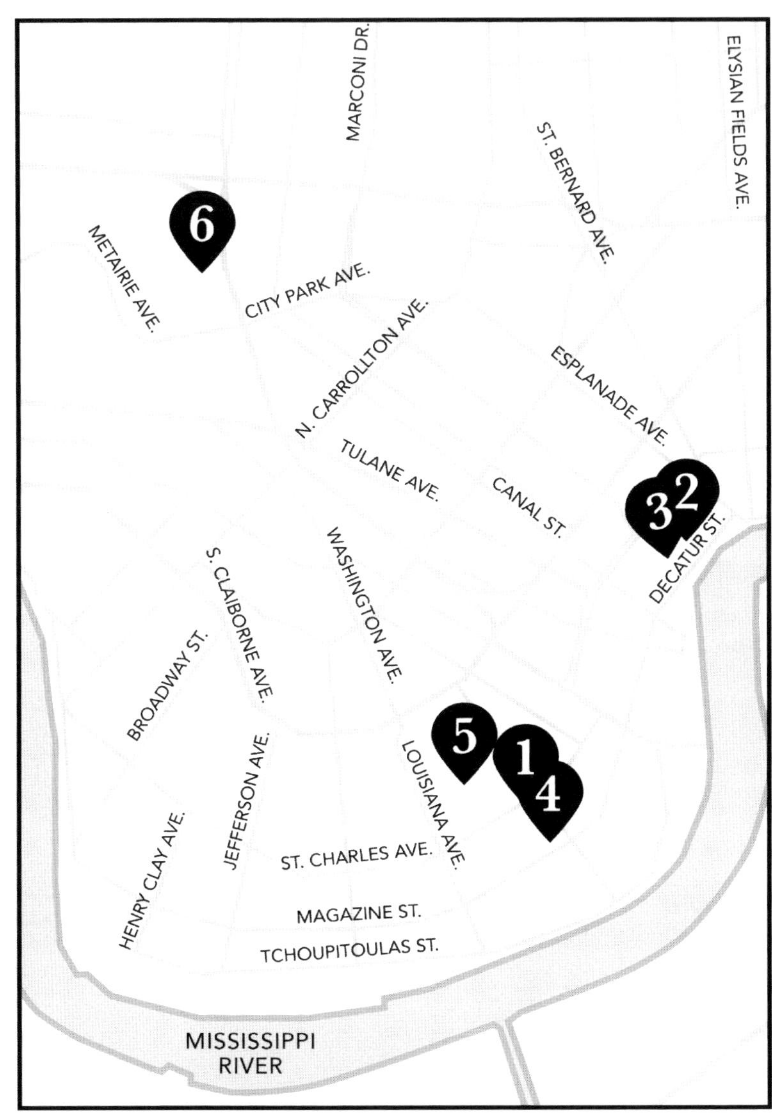

1 Anne Rice's Orphanage Home, 2301 St. Charles Avenue
2 Vampire Café, 801 Royal Street
3 The Dungeon Bar, 738 Toulouse Street
4 Anne Rice's house, 1239 First Street
5 Lafayette Cemetery, 2110 Washington Avenue
6 Metairie Cemetery, 5100 Pontchartrain Boulevard

8

VAMPIRES CLIMB OUT OF RUPTURED TOMBS

ASSUMING DEATH IN LIFE: NEW ORLEANS VAMPIRES

What makes a woman slip inside a glass casket? Throw her own jazz funeral? Climb out of a coffin to attend her own book signing? It's preposterous, this idea of vampires and the cemeteries that launched them.

Corpses don't leave the grave at night to drink the blood of the living, bite their necks with long, pointed canine teeth. Or do they?

New Orleans's own Anne O'Brien Rice[130] was drawn to death in life. Was she pulled to Lafayette Cemetery because of its ghosts? Her vampires ruptured from their tombs. She chronicled over one hundred vampires. Her goal was to make you believe that imaginary beings, like Lestat and Louis, are *real.*

Like the rain, we keep expecting vampires. These nocturnal creatures lurk in cemeteries, crypts, trees. If we spend the night in Lafayette Cemetery or the BK House, where *Interview with the Vampire* was filmed, will we feel the undead? Spot vampires climbing out of caskets, biting the necks of the unsuspecting?

Don't we yearn for vampire lovers to lift us off the bed, twirl us in their arms? Who touch us with their chiseled faces, their thick, loose hair. Whose wild-eyed stare consumes us. Don't we crave someone who nuzzles our neck? Dances chest to chest? Stares at us, sweet and soft?

So many of us haven't been touched. We struggle to cast our eyes down, to squeeze our legs together, to cuddle a body pillow. We crave someone who never denies their feelings, whose gaze never strays from ours.

Stop. Vampires don't exist.

Still, hypothetically, wouldn't you like to become one? To never die. To live in New Orleans forever. Be greeted by a spray of sweet juicy orchids on a table. Feel the spongy Oriental rugs under foot. Swing on the balcony. Taste the wetness of the air. Watch New Orleans tilt up at night: Mississippi River, Jackson Square, the Cathedral.

No. We don't want to talk about becoming vampires. No *body* outlives death. Stolen and drained blood can't revive a corpse. A cadaver decomposes within hours. Bloats and discolors within days.

Vampires are not real. And you can't become one.

Yes, but we desire for vampires to be real. Ghosts move though crumbling plaster walls, sail through stiff, crusty oak trees. Why can't vampires?

RECLAIMING THE DEAD AT ANNE RICE'S ORPHANAGE HOME

Anne Rice's Gothic home at 1239 First Street became the home of the Mayfair witches. Why do the wealthy buy property in the Garden District? Why does tragedy confront them before or after they do? What sorrows do residents struggle with in their mansions, inherited or bought?[131]

Anne wrote in the grips of agony for her dead child. She searched for meaning in her soulless universe.[132]

Her five-year-old died of leukemia, a blood disorder. She transformed her dead child, nicknamed Mouse, into the child vampire Claudia in her books. (She swears it was done unconsciously, though she had developed an obsessive interest in blood.)

Anne also presided over an opulent estate behind lush banana trees, blocks away from McGehee's School for Girls and the Consul General of France on Prytania Street.[133] She revamped this Second Empire–style orphanage on Napoleon Avenue, glamorizing this girls' Catholic orphanage built in 1865. She transformed it into fifty thousand square feet of luxury and continued birthing one imaginary vampire after the next.

Anne eulogized her daughter by creating a doll museum. The first residents were nondescript dolls, tattered and frayed, from the 1970s, when Mouse died. The collection grew with Anne's own rare and unique dolls, some over five feet tall. Dolls that had appeared in her novels joined the shelves. At night, did Anne's phantoms pull the dolls off the shelves and dance with them?

Anne reimagined the orphanage into a landmark, with ballrooms, quarters for her family, a bit of paradise. Was more tragedy on the way?

As the mansion expanded and glorified its ghostly doll residents, Anne's husband slipped toward a massive stroke. Anne left the mansion when he died. She couldn't live alone in gigantic quarters with just her genius. She eventually auctioned off her dolls, sold all her property, abandoned New Orleans for Southern California. There, she joined her son, Christopher, in the land of dreams.

The Vampire Mother's passing in 2021 shook New Orleans. We miss Anne Rice, her outrageous grandeur, her curiosity that drove her to inhabit the phantoms of her imagination. Will anyone replace the loss of genius creative Anne Rice?

DRINKING BLOOD PUDDING AT THE NEW ORLEANS VAMPIRE CAFÉ

What should we do to mourn Anne Rice? Let's revive ourselves with the finest food.

Slurp blood pudding at the New Orleans Vampire Café on Royal Street. (Blood pudding is sausage made from slaughtered animal blood. It tastes just like filet mignon that is served bloody rare.) We savor blood orange crème brûlée, blot our mouths with bat-shaped napkins.

Will we meet New Orleans's first vampire here? Jacques St. Germain[134] (one vampire mentioned before Anne Rice's pantheon of the undead) has been reappearing since the early 1900s. It's said he still lives on 1041 Royal Street, just two blocks away from us. Gorgeous (though violent, gory, depraved), Jacques once entertained lavishly. He seized and bit women in the neck, left bloodstains and wine bottles filled with blood. It's said he soared from a window and vanished.

Real vampires abound in New Orleans, linger inside doorways, thrive at night, socialize in private vampire clubs (like the New Orleans Vampire Association). They slither into forbidden places in the Quarter and arrive masked to vampire balls.

Will they jump out and grab our necks? Secure their fangs in our jugular veins? Levitate us off the ground? Probably not.

TOASTING VINEGAR WINE AT THE DUNGEON: NEW ORLEANS'S SECRET VAMPIRE BAR

Let's raise our glasses to the Vampire Queen and search for living vampires in her honor.

We're headed to New Orleans's secret vampire bar. We fly past art galleries on Toulouse Street, smile awkwardly at bikers who skulk by their row of black Harley Davidsons, wave at tourists tossing Mardi Gras beads from balconies in July.

We find a tiny, creepy alleyway to the Dungeon and then shuffle through this eerie entryway to find the blood suckers. Knock thrice on the prison cell door.

First thought (Rory): definitely should've worn the combat boots and black leather pants—not the pink lace dress and sandals.

First thought (Rosary): How long can I stay here and survive? How far will I go to write a book with my daughter?

Shackles hang like curtains. Strangers linger in elevated wooden cages above. They stare hungrily at the prey. Our names are Rosary, but you cannot pray on us.[135]

New Orleans is vampire obsessed. Who are these psychic vampires?

We clink our glasses of vinegar wine, soothe our sorrows with a vampire's kiss cocktail. But we keep an eye out for psychic vampires who try to make you believe they are real. Some wear fangs and perform blood-letting rituals. They *sip* a little blood. Sexual energy fuels most.

We wonder: is the fierceness of a vampire rooted in pain? Does trauma drive them to live in dark corners?

Like Anne Rice, many vampires identify as outsiders—not part of the community. But would Anne go out late at night on the prowl for a drink, an adventure and maybe even a vampire? No. She was too obsessed birthing vampires and generating her own outrageous worlds. All Anne did was write, write, write. And when she was tired, she wrote some more. She kept herself isolated. Many local artists (like us) tried to get her involved, but no one could break into that cage of her creativity. She was a titan—*invisible*, like her vampires.

Did Anne join the literati—Rowan and the Mayfair Witches—and the tombs used in her vampire series?[136] How wonderful that the lavish Lafayette Cemetery (if a cemetery can be lavish) was just blocks from the mansion.

No, she pulled up stakes from her Lafayette Cemetery, where her monstrous creatures panted. She retreated to the suburbs. She found her

The Dungeon Beckons. Photograph by Rachelle O'Brien.

Left: *Halloween*. *Photograph by Cheryl Gerber.*

Below: *Metairie Cemetery, Anne Rice. Photograph by Cheryl Gerber.*

final spot in Metairie Cemetery, the death place locals dream of, marked with a black cross on her tomb door.[137]

All we have left of Anne is her mausoleum, tagged "RICE," at the T-junction of Avenue Bell and Avenue O in Metairie Cemetery, near Millionaire's Row. A plot of grass surrounds her Greco-Roman tomb. There are no giant grieving statues, no wraparound galleries, no drooping oak trees, no palms, no palmettos, no palace. No flowers embellish the tomb—just parched grass, sky and sun.

Anne rests in her one-room tomb with her husband and baby daughter. She awaits her Christopher. He is now making film adaptations of Anne's books, helping us dream that Lestat and the others crouch around the bend.

Where do Louis, Claudia and her other vampires go, now that their inspiratrix has left? Do her vampires come looking for their mother? Can her princes be spotted lurking in nearby crypts and elaborate aboveground marble tombs? Do they find solace in cemetery statues that weep, move and groan? Are sneaky vampires hiding out in her vault, waiting for someone or something to revive them?

Anne Rice's death still bites those who knew her. Only her 40 books, which have sold over 150 million copies, remain. (In the beginning was *The Word*, lest we forget the power of that.) Anne Rice was worth $60 million when she died.

Now, the Queen of the Vampires is gone. Like Bram Stoker, the Irishman who created Dracula, Anne Rice is turning into dust. Let's remember Anne the way she was when she created the New Orleans vampires, these beloved sensitive, glamorous literary monsters: smart, clever, invincible—except for this need for blood.

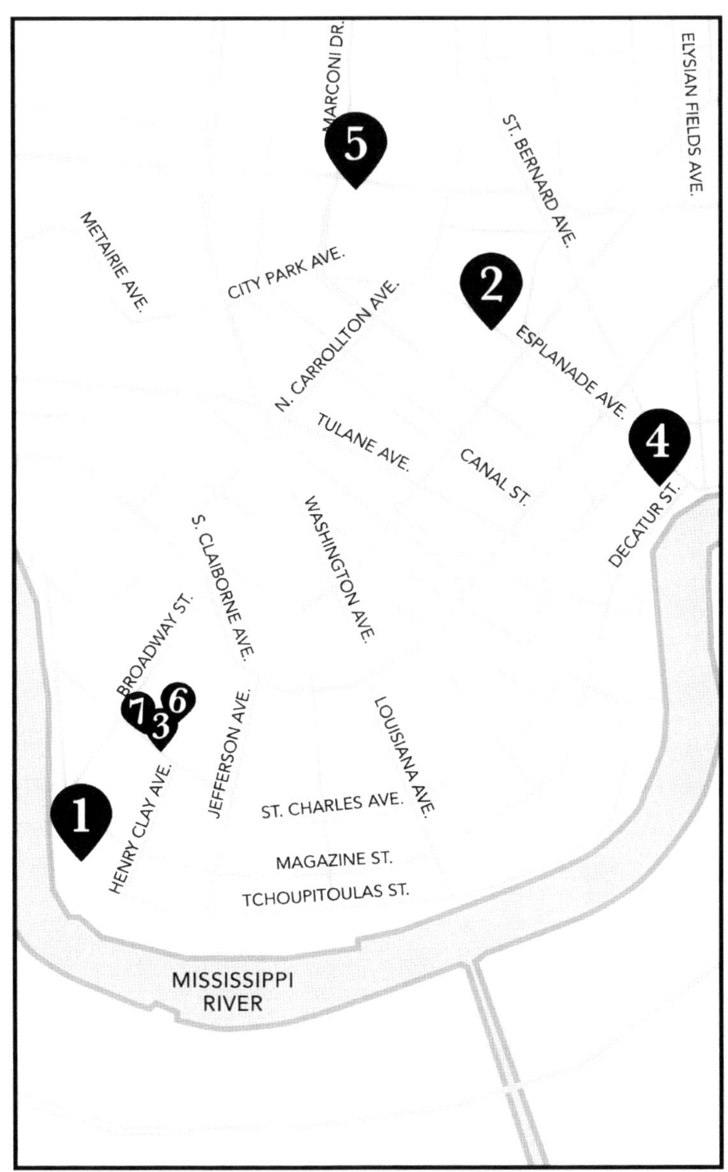

1 Audubon Park, 6500 Magazine Street
2 Estelle Degas' House, 2918 Esplanade Avenue
3 The Buchner House, 6330 St. Charles Avenue
4 De la Vergne House, 823 Esplanade Avenue
5 City Park, 1 Palm Drive
6 Loyola University, 6363 St. Charles Avenue
7 Tulane University, 6823 St. Charles Avenue

9

GROWING UP HAUNTED

UPTOWN NEW ORLEANS AND THE GARDEN DISTRICT

All the houses Uptown are haunted.

UPTOWN SWARMS WITH GHOSTS

It almost feels sacrilegious to say ghosts don't exist Uptown. But why is Uptown flooded with ghosts?[138] Maybe it's because water from the Mississippi River conducts energy from the spirit world.

Water magnetizes ghosts. They need to absorb strength from whatever they can. Uptown invites a powerful draw.[139]

Some Uptown spirits manifest as full-bodied apparitions; others are partial-bodied. Some show themselves as orbs. Some appear as dark shadows that are seven feet tall. Some wear a hat. Some can't remember what their body looked like, what they were dressed in when they died.

Uptown swings about two Gothic universities, with their expansive, luscious and verdant campuses.[140] Beauty magnetizes even the dead. Grecian mansions and massive homes with turrets—do spirit creatures scratch to get out? Can you make out their cries and whimpers from fireplaces?

Ghosts abound in sensuous Audubon Park, twist around oak trees, hide inside bearded moss, slither into lagoons, chase egrets, mallards, little blue herons. If spirits could stretch out their ghost arms over the capacious park, they'd create a shroud over two thousand trees, half of which are native live oaks.[141]

Walk Among the Giants. Photograph by Rachelle O'Brien.

We love Uptown because it feels timeless, with its giant houses with steep roofs, long shuttered windows boarded tight, eyes closed to the world, ghost-like. Its small, squat cottages sit by the river. Creole cottages, shotgun,[142] doubles and camelback houses fill this neighborhood.[143]

So many secrets are hidden in those palm-draped front yards with droopy elephant ears and lush *Alice in Wonderland*–like greenery. Let go, and you will fall through a rabbit hole into this mystic neighborhood. Blue, pink, green, yellow, purple, tomato, poppy houses, all turn black and ominous when rain falls—and every evening when the ghosts come out.

When sunlight fades, do you dare walk the riverside of Saint Charles Avenue and creep Uptown, gawk at the estates? Don't you know rats crouch inside these banana trees? Tiger cats scream from windows. German shepherds prowl the yards. What do their eyes see that we don't?

Step with us into a residential area: Jeanette Street south of Carrollton Avenue. (This is the major road Uptown that connects with Saint Charles Avenue). Peek through tall Victorian windows. Figures appear and disappear in the shadows of low-burning chandeliers and globe lanterns. Dim light makes the forms glow.

Overhead, oak limbs stretch across the avenue, trying to touch each other. The drooping branches are pregnant with ghosts.

These spirits go back to 1874, when the towns of Lafayette and Carrollton were absorbed into the city. Are they part of the doomed families who were crushed inside these buildings? Ghosts come to the wealthy and the poor, in fancy parts of Uptown and in failing parts by the river and everything in between. All these shotgun houses, bungalows and cottages have their ghost stories. We've heard them.

A New Orleans Ghost Tale: The Nurse Ghost

Ghosts awakened when their graves were dug up under our Uptown house for the construction of an addition. The excavation's effect was like turning this haunted house's volume level to max.

Construction roused a ghost nurse from her slumber. She visited my parents in their newly built bedroom. Mom woke up terrified and cold and felt the presence of someone at the foot of her bed. She pried open her eyes. The ghost was dressed in a wartime nurse's uniform with a blue veil. She was floating and had no lower body, just the upper parts. Mom reached over to wake up Dad. They looked over, but the nurse was gone.

Later, Dad was sick in bed; he had walking pneumonia. He woke up when the linen closet door opened. The war nurse ghost exited, walked across the room and then went out the back door. He could make out the details of her face, see how wrinkled her face was. In a state of shock, he shuffled out his bedroom. Our family was having dinner and stopped. He was so pale.

My older sister said, "Dad, you look like you've seen a ghost."

He replied, "I have."

This city seethes with ghosts. Are we walking in their footsteps, hearing their whispers, feeling their presence?

Do some ghosts have some strong emotions of the past—remorse, fear or terror of a violent death—associated with them? Probably. Some died with strong negative emotions, which linger into the afterlife. The living perceive their heavy or oppressive energy. What happens if the ghosts try to communicate, and their attempts are not understood? Further distress. A manifestation of negative energy.

Yes, children died young and unexpected in old Uptown, baby boys with block haircuts and ringlets, girls in red plaid smocked dresses. Many passed away under the age of six and were buried in white gowns. Were they in carriage accidents, diseased, poisoned or shot?

Metairie Cemetery, Moriarty Monument. Photograph by Cheryl Gerber.

Our doctor told us that her kids repeatedly witness ghost children in her Uptown house and yard. (Children have a heightened sensitivity and perceive ghostly presences that adults might miss, discount and even defy.) A phantom toddler pedaled a ghost tricycle into their dining room. Other apparitions rode the slide, jumped on the seesaw, climbed into the treehouse. Playful ghosts like to toy with the living. They steal a spoon. Sometimes, they give it back. Sometimes, they don't.

We bite our lips. Do we really want to move into haunted stories of Uptown homes?

What sorrows do these parents live with in their mansions, either inherited or bought? Survivors march through the pain in New Orleans, teens we loved and lost. One starved herself to death in her debutante year. A boy was beheaded in a car wreck. Another died while escaping his attic bedroom using sheets.

The wealthy defied life. Then they were silenced in mausoleums in Metairie Cemetery. But do angry teenage spirits spiral back to their family mansions? Smoke weed on the side porch? Take the Jaguar convertible for a spin? Hide their father's shoes?

Some New Orleans teens have been groomed from an early age, performing in ballet, gymnastics, soccer, ballroom dancing, golf, fencing, sailing, skiing, horseback riding and social clubs (8 o'clocks for eighth grade dances). They know all the social graces and can slalom ski, win a sailing regatta at the Southern Yacht Club or a golf tournament at the Country Club. Are these ghosts haunting us?

Look for their ghosts leaning over balconies. One hand holds a silver goblet full of chipped ice. The other hand waves to throw Mardi Gras beads.

The presence of ghosts is hard to prove—and disprove. But in the old parts of New Orleans, the veil between the living and the dead is the thinnest. Especially at dusk. Spirits haunt where they used to live. Because really, if you love your home, why would you want to leave it?

Here in New Orleans, ghosts reside below us, next to us and above us in the oak trees. Our commitment to gaining more knowledge about our haunted hometown keeps us up at night. It ignites our third eye, fuels our imagination. Are we becoming wiser philosophers, researchers, seekers? Or are we losing our grip of reality and falling into the crevasse of death obsession? You decide.

A New Orleans Ghost Tale: Lost Ghost in the Bathroom

One day, I got home. I walked in the kitchen, and I felt: "Something's wrong." The screen door was off the hinge. "Something's not right." I had left the doors unlocked, so I thought there must be an intruder in the house.

I grabbed a knife, which is so stupid. (Why didn't I leave? I have no idea.) I started looking around the house. Under the bed. Everywhere in the house. No one was there. Then I realized: "The bathroom. Someone's in the bathroom."

Outside the bathroom door, I called out, "Hey, if you're in here, you have to get out." I hear—as clear as day—a male voice say, "What's going on?" He sounded terrified.

I'm thinking: "Oh my God, is he on drugs? This guy is confused, right? He got lost. He went in the wrong house."

Instead of just leaving, I decided to go into the bathroom. I took a deep breath, this butcher knife in my hand. I opened the door. No one was in there.

I'm thinking: "Oh my God, he's in the bath. He's in the shower." So, I walked over to the shower curtain with this knife, shaking. I'm thinking: "What am I about to do—kill somebody?"

I tear back the curtain there. No one *was there.*

THE CHIC DEAD IN THE GARDEN DISTRICT

We head down to the Garden District, where we can't help but sense the ghosts. We've got to keep moving. The place is ghost patrolled. As the light dims, will you make out apparitions?

We step lightly among the elite, knowing that we don't belong in the Garden District.[144] We misfits are unable to enter these gated estates with their drooping palmettos. We can't ease our Cadillac into a private garage, nod at the security patrol. We tiptoe past luscious courtyards, where wild parrots squawk and glimmer in ancient oak trees.[145] Persian cats caterwaul in windows. Angst-ridden privileged teens rage on black-laced balconies. Toothy German shepherds growl behind cast-iron fences.[146]

Don't stop to inhale the scent of honeysuckle on tall cornstalk fences. Can't you see the apparition on the other side of the wrought-iron gate?

You can't evade ghosts in New Orleans. Our advice? *Keep moving.*

The light dims. You don't have *time* to cradle a pulpy magnolia. Ghosts patrol the Garden District.

Fog descends. Skip past the bruised ghost rocking on her porch chair, squeezing the arm rests with her skinless hands. Does she even want to visit family anymore? The living are ripping with rage.

Lamplight blurs. What are those twenty-somethings doing over there, idling on the gallery? Are they real? Are they toying with a razor? Clicking a gun? Are they—or will they soon be—dead?

One hundred quick heartbeats: that's likely what you'll experience if you walk at dusk. Strolling past those Gothic mansions and the ghostly banana trees drooping in front of them, you'll see the violent crows, overgrown fences and the galleries streaked with shadows.

Step inside these glorious decaying mansions and Creole cottages, and you may glimpse the edge of a ghost's gown in the doorway as she skirts out of the room. There's so much Victorian furniture that spirits forget the home is no longer theirs. There are so many armoires that the minute you knock on them, you fear someone will knock back.

Sometimes, they do.

Not too far away, Esplanade Avenue's oldest section, from Decatur Street to Rampart Street, runs alongside the French Quarter. The double row of oaks reach their arms over Esplanade Avenue. Are they weeping or crying out in anguish?

The avenue opens up from its tunnel of trees to deliver you into City Park.[147] The district boasts one of the largest concentrations of historic buildings in the United States. Some are redone. Some are quietly deteriorating. Some are breathing restlessly.

Let's sneak inside a possessed mansion. Maybe we'll find a woman's corpse wrapped up inside drapery, an elderly person poisoned, keeled over in the butler's pantry, or a dead man in a tuxedo, collapsed from a heart attack, hidden under a tablecloth so the party could go on. This is the Big Easy, the Fun City, the City that Care Forgot.

In the bedrooms, ghost women move about unseen—women who drank themselves into comas while their husbands bedded their best friend downstairs. You can feel the grief in their brief appearances. Vacant stares. Bodiless footsteps. Mysterious whimpers. A wry look, between amusement and regret snares their faces.

They open the armoires, slide inside the silk gowns, white minks, cashmere scarves and velvet capes. They twist up their hair, apply makeup to skeleton faces, preserve themselves, even if a hand is missing or their arm is just a bone.

GOOD GHOSTS RETURNING: ESTELLE DEGAS, MUSE OF EDGAR DEGAS

Is Esplanade Avenue haunted? Yes, this former Millionaire's Row for the city's Creole community lives and breathes ghosts.[148] They're in its violently colored and pale mansions and weeping oak trees, drooping down to claw at the neutral ground. They're in its wispy, thick air, all the way from one end of the wicked Mississippi down to the gasping gators of Bayou Saint John. People who redo the mansions with fine antiques, John James Audubon bird images and oil portraits, often fear these ghosts. Many feel dark presences in their massive hallways, libraries, billiards rooms and chandeliered bedrooms.[149]

Bywater View. Photograph by Robert Schaefer Jr.

We sail down Esplanade Avenue to one famous ghost in residence,[150] Estelle Musson Degas, the sister-in-law (and first cousin)[151] of the famous painter Edgar Degas. The beautiful, blind Estelle was a mother of seven whose husband[152] betrayed her with her best friend, expelled her from his world.

Pity the ghosts, won't you? The broken ones may whimper—even legendary ones, brave heroines, like Estelle. She buried five of her children—heart-wrenching. Is her spirit unresolved? Estelle's body revolted each time she laid a child in a casket. In death, does she relive their loss?

Some say Estelle prowls her sad two-bedroom cottage on Bayou Saint John. Does she move about, no longer blind, pushing through the pocket doors, her hoop skirt whipping past the fireplace?

Small items disappear. Is Estelle taking a little vial of perfume for Jo, struck dead in her debut year? Does she pocket a toy for Pierre? (Both

A NEW ORLEANS GHOST TALE: THE DEMENTOR

A dark shadow was lurking in the corner of my room. It gave me the chills.

One night, this demon showed himself. He floated through the air in black tattered robes like a dementor.

I woke up in midair. I was thrown out of my bed—literally thrown. *I hit the glass door and then fell on the ground.*

I invited my church friend, who is a youth leader, to help. She blessed different parts of my home with anointing oil. Made the sign of the cross. Prayed. Opened the doors and windows. Commanded the spirit to leave: "In the name of Jesus Christ, you cannot be here."

succumbed to scarlet fever.) Or maybe she's looking for a baby bracelet for Jeanne, vanquished by yellow fever? Will she massage cream on their decaying fingers tonight?

The current owners of this house hear small footsteps. They say Estelle returns, disrupts the house when men enter—she's eternally suspicious. Her wounds from betrayal persist.

Does Estelle float down the street to the New Orleans Museum of Art, where her portrait reigns? New Orleanians led her portrait's campaign: Bring Estelle Home. Well, home is where she will stay.

Perhaps she stands before this Degas painting in the second-floor gallery, sees herself again with hopeful eyes, pregnant before the deaths began, before she dove into herself and claimed her greatest power.

If you see dear Estelle, please don't look into her eyes. If she sees you, she'll vanish.

HAUNTED HAPPENINGS IN HISTORIC HOUSES

What other families of ghosts are chained to the New Orleans in the afterlife?

We zip over to the Buchner House (built in 1856)[153] on Jackson Avenue to see the ghost midwife. Will Josephine appear and vanish in the shadows? She rushes from room to room, turns the lights off and on, opens and closes doors, sways the chandelier. Why is Josephine still haunting this mansion? Who is the ghost child, whose soft cries echo behind her?

Shadows strangle the Corinthian columns and massive wraparound veranda at the Mansión Magnolia on 2127 Prytania Street. The same architect who crafted Anne Rice's sinister mansion on 1239 First Street built this one. The *undead* love it! Gracious ghost hosts welcome you,[154] latch and unlatch the doors for you, dull the chandelier when it's too bright.

We listen for small ghost feet running up and down the stairs. We are poised to catch shadows flickering in the corner. We hold our purses tight. We don't want to invite ghost children to run off with our new makeup. We hope the innocent child who drowned doesn't introduce herself.[155] When she opens her mouth to speak, water pours out.

Don't expect to sleep here. If you feel a cool breeze skate across your cheek around 3:00 a.m., keep your eyes closed. A ghost is stroking your face. One friend shared a similar ghost encounter: "Lights start to flicker. I feel a ghost stroking my arm. Then it keeps coming up. Hostile. Wants to overtake me."

Let's shake it off, shall we? We stroll over to the De las Vergne House on Esplanade and Burgundy. Listen for golf balls smashing against the walls—that's Jules. He has wild black hair, tight lips. He smashes the golf ball with the correct angle of attack, direction and speed. Walls shake. Tenants have tried to stop him, but he vanishes. Does he think he still owns the place? Is he driven to punish some perpetrator, violator, fiend? Is it his brother-in-law, who bludgeons his wife?

Time to go. The outdoors will be safer, under the canopy of mother nature's arms.

BAD SPIRITS INCITING VIOLENCE: THE SUICIDE AND DUELING OAKS

We head to City Park, searching for solace under those giant live oaks. We arrive early in the morning (before we can talk ourselves out of it). We shuffle under the oaks, absorb the sunlight shooting through their branches. But we feel unsafe in this damp, shady location. We sense a menacing presence underfoot.

There *are* evil spirits in City Park, these hundred acres of which John McDonogh donated to the city in 1850. Lord knows, those ancient trees have witnessed strife, pain and death.

Do ghosts fly through the lagoons, palmettos, crepe myrtles and sycamores in City Park? Do fleeing spirits rush into voluminous oaks, needing to hide?[156] Do they roll up inside the thick trunks of eight-hundred-year-old bearded oaks?

Two mortuary spots thrive within these fierce trees: the Suicide and Dueling Oaks, remnants of this primordial forest. With a long lifespan and mighty presence, these trees may be havens for the dead. Are their hollowed-out trunks of the oaks large enough to shelter ghost families?

Anger rages inside these scorned oaks, sinking into the earth. They whisper back and forth inside their scabby bark. Their skin is crisped so gray they can barely lift their limbs. Some may have to be propped up with poles.

At the end of Esplanade Avenue looms the Suicide Oak, like a bad digestif. Hopeless men in the nineteenth century ended their lives dangling below these 120 feet spread branches. Limp, they couldn't look up at the tree's 58-foot height as they fell unconscious. They couldn't hug its 24-foot belly.

Do the undead come out of the slimy lagoons with their slippery snakes and alligators? (Do they slink back there when the night ends?) Do the ghosts of those who ended their own lives grunt, bellow, splash around on top of gators, eyes glowing red at night? Are they trying to forget who they are and enjoy themselves? Like reptiles, do they see better at night?

Suicide Oak. Photograph by Rachelle O'Brien.

Bridges in Time, City Park. Photograph by Rachelle O'Brien.

Will confused phantoms emerge, trying to make sense of what happened? Do they condemn those brackish Medusa-like trees for their hand in death?

A soldier, a boy on a crutch, a cotton factor with a rope, do they keep looking for their watch, their wallet or any object they feel they shouldn't have dropped? Some died so suddenly that they don't realize they're dead. Hanging can choke off a person's blood in two seconds. Brain cells start to die after two minutes; after ten, too few remain to resume life.

Sixteen men hanged themselves here. Did any kiss their mother or sister goodbye? Or did they just leave their homes with all lights on, money on the desk, window open, as if they were coming back? Did they leave a note? Did someone have to call their fathers to come cut their lifeless bodies down? Take their corpses to Odd Fellows Rest?

Who were they, so desperate that they hanged themselves in a public park, where children picnic, couples paddle on swan boats and old folks chatter?

No. We're not going to identify your names. Make you famous for deeds that tortured others the rest of their lives. Relatives went to bed screaming, eyes puffed with tears, beating themselves up for not stopping a husband or a son, not predicting the sorrow in his dragging, slow eyes and pained grin.

It's all so merciless for the poor ones who remain. They have to send out the black-rimmed announcements. Find a ready plot. Notify others with the sobbing news. Bag up clothes. Pay off bills. Close the already depleted bank accounts.

The air feels dense. Oh my, what's that groaning and whispering? Are spirits watching us? No one else is present in the park. Something flickered over there. Aren't ghosts supposed to hide till night, when there's more energy for them to look about?

Some coldness blends with the humidity. It takes a lot of energy for ghosts to manifest. If they don't have much, they attach to the living, fuel off their energy. That's why it's so cold everywhere ghosts go. A New Orleans filmmaker friend warned us: "Places aren't haunted; people are." Beware: ghosts can attach to you, no matter where you go.

Out of the corner of our eyes, we see shadows flicker, leaves rustle. Dense mats of moss tremble, as if many eyes are watching us.

We pray *no* ghosts emerge—not this morning, not before coffee.

They're tortured souls. We feel their draining presence. And the air so cold and sharp that our joints stiffen. But it's too late. We don't want them pulling at us. So, what if they are not ready to move on—they can't accept their passing and need to deliver a message. We cry for them. But we don't know how to help them with their soft, sagging eyes, their unbuttoned jackets, sagging mouths, sheepish grins.

We are not their mothers, sisters, lovers. They took their own lives, and we are two centuries too late. They can't keep coming back. We know death isn't the end of everything, but they're supposed to be turning to *dust*!

Careful if you race out of this place. The Dueling Oak stands just one hundred feet away.[157] You don't want to step on some piece of bloody ground and deface something. Call a dead dueler back. Summon a spirit that survives underground.

This ominous oak stretches seventy feet high and twenty-five feet wide. It has dominated City Park for three hundred years. (Two dueling oaks existed until a hurricane knocked one down in 1949.)

Duels were so common in this park that nobody would try to stop the challenges, and they might even draw a crowd.[158] It was considered an honor to defend your wife, your family, but it was also a dangerous act. Duelers might become maimed, crippled—or killed. Although police started breaking up duels in 1855, the conflicts secretly continued.

Dueling was so rapid. On the count of three, challengers would shoot. And men would duel for all kinds of trivial and foolish reasons, like a supposed betrayal, a misplaced sneer. One duel was the result of a man placing his chair too close to another man's sister at a dinner party. A doctor could be present at the duel, but could he, with his little physician's bag, truly save anyone?

Are the vanquished combatants flagrant, floppy, derelict? Do they sob under live oak trees, too far gone in the darkness of death to grieve their sins? Do restless spirits wail at night, asking for mercy for having either killed or been killed?

Is the bark of that tree moving? Let's go closer. Hold your breath. One step at a time. Oh no, that's a man's face twisting inside the bark.

Shhh. Don't tell the duelists we're here. We don't want any ghost to suspect we'll claim their lost treasure—spectacles, coins or rings.

Something brushes past us. Do you hear that moaning, booing and knocking? Oh, my goodness, they are everywhere. Invisible shadows are on the ground. It's not just the sun going down.

There's a sharp breeze, like a slap. Do you see that? It could be the ghost of Pepe Lulla, armed with his sword. It takes evil to look straight at someone and saber them in the eye or the chest. So many people were killed, the city had to build St. Vincent DePaul Cemetery to bury them.

Would you, if you had killed dozens, want to come back to the scene of the crime? Would you beg God on your hands and knees to lift you out of some worse hell?

We don't want Pepe bursting through that tree, charging, roaming the park like a mad dog. Cry out: "Fight, slaughter, win!" We don't want to wrestle with the devil.

His followers, the Defiants, could be close. Not all ghosts come back to grieve their sins. Keep your distance, their weapons could be real or imagined. We're in a world of the ghost bandits.

Glowing orbs appear at the dueling oak near dusk. Maybe those are good spirits? Let's not wait and find out.

Run!

10

A GHOSTLY FAREWELL

Forgive us, dear reader. We must stop writing about ghosts—for now. We hate to abandon you. We've reached our limit.

We're sorry. We need to author serious books next—historical fictions, novels, books on American history and art.

We can't be labeled phantom authors. We're married to serious scientists. What will the world think of our PhDs now?

We're academics. We can't be branded *horror* writers. *We'll never get promoted.* We're visiting Fulbright scholars. Won't we be crucified if we remain in the world of spirits and *possession*?

We can't tremble at night anymore, sleep with all the lights on, hide with our heads under our sheets, wear sleep masks to blind ourselves and earplugs to deafen ourselves, drape the bed with rosaries, reach for mother of pearl crucifixes in our top drawers.

When a ghost arrives in our bedrooms at 3:00 a.m., we refuse to treat him like the living. We won't ask, "How can I help you?" *No.* We do not want to help a ghost with his trauma. We won't open a portal to the next world.

No more. No more demons at the window. No more visons and sleep paralysis. No more group hallucinations of a poltergeist. No more spiritual warfare.

We are not interested in meeting some nonhuman being that lingers in the darkness. *No, thank you.*

We evict the specters behind us in the mirror. We command the headless monk or suicide nun: "Stay in the attic or the hidden rooms—not in the halls!"

We don't want to leave more letters and gifts in the attic for little Rebekah, who died in a house fire. Wake up to a little girl ghost holding our hand. Asking, "Why am I dead?"

We don't want to freeze in terror while a dementor stares at us, throws us against the wall. (Do demons harass people? We should have researched them before taking on this book. But we were too scared.)

By showing an interest in ghosts, did we accidentally invite them to come closer?

We never should have started this ghost thing. Our legs tremble. We stabilize.

Do you hear us? Are we getting through to somebody?

In the silence, we feel an energy building, a knocking sound. We sit up in the bed. In the middle of the night, the mattress shifts. A peaceful nun wearing a velvet tunic with a hood sits down. She has grandma energy. We stare into her face under her hood. What do we see? A universe of darkness.

Spirits crave deep connection, empathy, possession, closure. Others demand vindication, destruction, revenge. Which one will you become?

In different parts of New Orleans—the Bywater, the Irish Channel, Uptown, the Marigny, the French Quarter, the Garden District—if you tune in, you'll feel a thickness in the air. An angriness. A contempt. A melancholy. An immortal longing. A ghostly presence.

Writing a ghost book has changed us. Our Irish grandmother's stories aren't fiction anymore. We don't need ghosts to burn our wrists to prove that *hell* is real.

Our dreams are transformed. Are the messages revelatory? Are they warnings? We don't know. But we feel in our bones the peels of thunder and lightning. A heavy cloud. Confusion.

Where are we—in a swamp? The edge of Metairie Cemetery? The sky turns red brown. We feel this invisible presence. *Oh lord, help us*. We're floating now.

A witch emerges, her face turns gray, her eyes roll back in her head. We sense malevolence. Our muscles tense. We clench our fists, wave them in the air. We try to say, "No evil." But the witch freezes our mouths *shut*. We use our hands, manually crack open our jaws. We command: *no evil*.

We're not going to leave you unprotected. We don't have all the answers—we have some. Remember to call on the good. Pray to the Divine. Bathe yourself in white light.

St. Louis Cathedral, Front. Pen and ink drawing by Billy Harris.

Call out dead relatives' names, "Michael, Mary, Theresa!" Then whisper friends' names, "Dawn, Herman, Mrs. Chisolhm!" Remember lost pets, "Ralphie, Ozzie, Bella, Tattoo!" Someone or something may be protecting you from the other side.

Say firmly, "Look. We don't even want to see loved ones. We don't need you to visit us to comfort us. Leave. We don't want you to make noises, flicker the lights, emit smells of roses."

We can't invite *ghosts* into our lives anymore. We are percolating creatives. We are too emotional, too prone to panic, *too*, *too*, *too*.

We hear a message in an ethereal, otherworldly voice: "Don't stop writing. Who will pass on our New Orleans stories?"

We will.

THE NEXT REALM

Dear readers, before we leave you, we will share sacred poetry and interviews with scholars and survivors—and just a few more tales of the undead.

THE SACRED UNSEEN: POETRY BY BARRET O'BRIEN

"THE WALKOVER"

But didn't we all end up
in the same corral?
All branded with the
same iron.
Politician or piano tuner.
Thief or thespian.
Aren't we all here, waiting
for our shearing before
flying naked into that
great gray fog.
And didn't I just forget
my credit rating and
my placement in the
one and only road race
I signed on to run?

"RETURNING TO DARKNESS"

after weeks away in cities
that never shut down,
the darkness around my house
is shocking, a bath of ice.
almost too holy to bear.

i want to grab it, encircle it,
wrap it safely in my arms,
tell the cities they can't have it,
these visible stars,
this absence of progress.

O! holy night.
O! sacred unseen.

"WAKING"

You think you're waking in your little bed,
in your little life,
destined to a morning of eggs and toast.
You think you're alone in a big fat ugly world
and that no one hears your words
or sees your eyes flutter when you speak to them.
Somehow you think that it's all gone bad,
and that the dreams you dreamt while you slept,
the ones that match like memory to your day,
are just happenstance,
blips on the radar,
circles in an otherwise perfect line of a life.
But to me,
from here,
you're pure light,
one-hundred trillion shots of life
stacking and standing so bright
I can't look at you directly.

To me,
you're part of a miracle so big
only your dreams can arrange it.
To me,
you're waking to a life
so potent,
that even you,
in your infinite modesty
may not be able to hold it back.

"SMOKE"

smoke makes a shadow.
didn't know that.
the aftereffects of fire
have their own presence.

"Sacred Hauntings"

Lyrics by Rachelle O'Brien and Eric Laws

Where have you gone?
Why can't I see?
Phantoms fly high.
They're all around me.

Love never dies.
There is no death.
My love immortal,
Take your last breath.

No need to fear.
The spirits fly free.
Protecting the living.
From things they can't see.

Sacred Hauntings,
All around me.

Flickering lights,
Electricity.
You let me know
Your presence is with me.

All around me.
All around me.

Heavy in the city.
You're so heavy in the city.
Heavy heavy in the city.
You're so heavy in the city.

Sacred Hauntings.
Sacred Hauntings.
Sacred Hauntings.
Sacred Hauntings.

EXPERTS AND AUTHORS REFLECT ON AMERICA'S MOST HAUNTED CITY

INTERVIEW WITH DR. C.W. CANNON

New Orleans History Professor, Loyola University, New Orleans

Scholar C.W. Cannon, PhD, has written, studied and taught New Orleans history and culture for decades. His books include *I Want Magic: Essays on New Orleans, the South, and Race*; *Soul Resin*; *Katrina Means Cleansing*; *French Quarter Beautification Project*; and *Sleepytime Down South*. His anthologies are *Louisiana in Words* and *Do You Know What It Means to Miss New Orleans*.

We spoke with Dr. Cannon to learn more about New Orleans's identity as a haunted city as part of its rich cultural inheritance. He shared locals' perspectives of ghosts (as well as his own) and the history of ghost literature in Louisiana.

WHY IS NEW ORLEANS AMERICA'S MOST HAUNTED CITY?

New Orleans is America's most haunted city for a reason. And I know other cities probably market themselves that way, but New Orleans is one of the major cities in the United States that has monetized its ghostly history, its ghostly past. New Orleans is a great candidate for being the ghost capital of the United States.

There are several places in the Quarter where there are ghost stories, and tales of suicides and murders. Often, they're having to do with the city's racial past.

The Ghosts Next Door. Photograph by Rachelle O'Brien.

There's a history of terror in New Orleans. Suffering. Unjust death. Maybe that's where ghosts come from.

I think New Orleans is haunted by its history. I think it is a very haunted place for lots of reasons. There's not this American impulse to bury the past. Forget about it. Move on brightly into the future.

New Orleans has always been about continuity, about trying to find some way to balance the future with a respect for the past and incorporating the past. That might be one reason why ghosts are so at home here.

This is a place that would welcome ghosts more than a shiny modern city, like Orlando, where it's all about the future that doesn't have this deep past....There's also a sense that death is with us. Death is coming.

WHAT ARE SOME NEW ORLEANIANS' PERCEPTIONS OF GHOSTS?

I think if you start talking, especially to middle class New Orleanians, they'll say, "All that ghost stuff is hyped for the tourists." But then there are a lot of people who say they've seen ghosts and believe in ghosts. Many who believe a lot of the ghost lore are especially more working-class background people, like people I went to school with in New Orleans public schools. And there's people like me, who see haunted New Orleans as a rich cultural inheritance.

HOW DID LOCALS SPEAK ABOUT HAUNTED PLACES WHEN YOU GREW UP IN NEW ORLEANS?

Growing up, everybody was talking about ghosts...There's a bunch of houses around where I grew up in the Marigny that were allegedly haunted. There were a lot more blighted structures than there are now. Now, it's been all fixed up and gentrified, but the blighted ones were boarded up and were rumored to be haunted. People would say, "Be careful."

We would creep in them and explore in the old broken-down houses, and that's always really kind of an evocative experience. You'd see like old items sitting on an old dresser that somebody left there. All of it seemed pregnant with the idea that it could be ghostly....

I would walk to school at McDonald 15 and would walk by Madame LaLaurie's mansion. Back then, I didn't know that's what it was. It was just a house and corner of Governor Nichols and Royal. I recall seeing people cross themselves when they went by it. So, I thought, "Is that a church or something?" Then somebody told me to be careful not to walk on that side of the street because that house was haunted. It was a very evil place.

WHAT IS THE HISTORY OF LITERATURE ON NEW ORLEANS GHOSTS?

There have been published ghost stories about the city going back a couple hundred years. George Washington Cable wrote *Strange True Tales of Louisiana* in the 1800s.

In the 1930s, and 1940s, people with the Federal Writers' Project collected stories, like *Gumbo Ya Ya* and *Folktales of Louisiana*. Evocative artwork and ghost stories of Louisiana have been collected, too.

It might be that ghost stories are expressing certain fears and wishes of people. In other words, ghost stories are metaphors for the way people feel about certain things....

There are old traditions of ghost stories in New Orleans that go back pretty much to the beginning. I think the African influence probably has a lot to do with that, too. A particular Africanized approach is to understand the presence of the ancestors as probable spirits....

I might direct you to a literary source: the poems of Brenda Maria Osby. *All Saints* is a beautiful collection of poems that won the American Book Award in 1998. She says she's very loving toward the dead in here. She says that our saints continue to live among us. She wrote a poem called "Peculiar Fascination with the Dead" that covers this in beautiful, poetic language. Basically, it's about the dead are with us here, and we accept them. We see them. We acknowledge them.

Brenda Maria Osby is from New Orleans. She's Afro Creole and she's very much coming out of the Black New Orleans literary tradition with an African perspective. The first section is called "Live Among Your Dead, Whom You Have Every Right to Love." She says that when we walk along those brick streets, our ancestors are in those bricks. Her vision of New Orleans as a haunted city is more of a loving vision than a scary, frightening vision. Our ancestors are among us. We love them. We love our dead people, and we honor them. One day we will join their ranks.

TELL US ABOUT SÉANCES IN NEW ORLEANS.

There is a tradition in New Orleans in the nineteenth century called spiritualism that was a very strong practice. Spiritualism is where you have séances to contact the spirits of the dead. They aren't exactly ghosts, but spirits.

A major Afro Creole fraternal organization in the nineteenth century was very active in politics in New Orleans. They had a beautiful hall there (that was also an event space where people would have concerts or weddings), where they had meetings. But also, they held séances in there. In their séances, they tried to contact their ancestors. They communed with their ancestors for advice about what to do in the present moment.

Spiritualism wasn't only in New Orleans; it happened throughout the United States in the late nineteenth century and in other countries, too, I imagine. In spiritualism, there's the belief in ghosts because you're contacting spirits of the deceased.

WHAT ARE NEW ORLEANIANS' PERSPECTIVES OF VOODOO?

You'll hear a lot from New Orleans people that Voodoo is just something to sucker the tourists. And then there's other people in New Orleans who, of course, practice Voodoo and believe in it.

WHAT DO YOU THINK—ARE GHOSTS REAL?

I've had experiences of feeling some strange presence. Being the very rational guy I am, I tend to assume that it's something in my unconscious that is causing me to experience something. But I don't know. I have enough intellectual humility to not preach that there's absolutely no chance that there's something like a ghost. I just don't know....

I believe all that stuff is possible. I think that it's very easy for us to project things from our unconscious into the world of perception. That doesn't surprise me at all. And people long for something beyond the visible world. I mean, that's what religion mostly is—the belief that there's a God out there—and people have a gut feeling that there's not. But that's a very upsetting feeling. So, they to escape that feeling of despair....

We're trained to distrust superstition, to reject superstition. Then sometimes it goes real far, and we reject myths altogether. New Orleans is, of course, a real capital of myth and superstition. It's magical. And some people react in a hostile way against that. I try to walk a tight rope by embracing the rich mythology of New Orleans. I think it's a rich cultural inheritance that all New Orleanians have ownership of.

INTERVIEW WITH MIKE HUBERTY

Founder of American Ghost Walks

American Ghost Walks provides tours in twenty-seven cities across the United States. We first met Mike when he invited us to speak about our book *New Orleans Voodoo: A Cultural Tradition* on his podcast *See You on the Other Side*. We interviewed Mike because we wanted to know why New Orleans is popular for ghost tourism. We were curious how this city's ghost tours connect to teaching history.

WHY ARE PEOPLE ATTRACTED TO HAUNTINGS IN NEW ORLEANS?

New Orleans obviously is the place for hauntings. The city has a fascinating history and a connection to culture that excites people. Talking about cultures that have a mystical aspect is thrilling. Many have a natural fascination with the unknown. It's the ultimate mystery—what happens after we die.

HOW DO GHOST TOURS CONNECT PEOPLE TO THE PAST?

Ghost tours really make you feel connected to a place in a different way than a normal history tour does. You don't get that feeling of the place and connection to things hundreds of years earlier, like you do in New Orleans.

When you're in certain parts of New Orleans, you're walking on steps or on bricks that were put in a couple of hundred years before. Families in town have been here for hundreds of years. Compare that to a place like Los Angeles, where a lot of the city is built in the early to mid-twentieth century. There's plenty of history but less of a sense of being transported in time. Walking the French Quarter feels like stepping into the past.

When you go to New Orleans and you talk about the history of the French, the Spanish, the English and the Louisiana Purchase, you add in an extra hundred years of history. Then you have the layer of the cross cultures coexisting, with the Cajuns and Africans.

We get in a mystical mood because there's an ancient feeling here, which you don't get in most of the United States. We all have a natural connection to something older than ourselves. The feeling of physically being in an ancient place like New Orleans automatically puts you in the mood where you can say to yourself: *OK, now we're in a place where something supernatural might happen.*

HOW ARE GHOST TOURS TIED TO TEACHING AMERICAN HISTORY?

History is the base layer on which ghost tour guides build the elements of the story that veer into the fantastic. We bring the listeners in with facts about New Orleans. Once we've established a grounded setting, we can let the ghost story take flight.

We share New Orleans legends and stories. We describe locals' experiences, the stories of people who go to work and live in these places

Haunted History Tours, Sidney Smith. Photograph by Cheryl Gerber.

every day. We connect this information to the history of the building, and the different people who lived there and worked there in the past (like Madame LaLaurie's mansion, which is in *American Horror Story*). Then we weave in the history of the land and of America. We also describe what was happening in the world at the time.

New Orleans ghost tours create a connection to the past that's more powerful than just your usual civics lesson. You're learning about New Orleanians' beliefs and experiences in the city, which feels more authentic.

MOTHER-DAUGHTER GHOST INTERVIEW

Dear readers, we want to share with you our ghost conversation: Daughter interviews mother.[159] Throw the kettle on. Prepare yourself a cup of Lady Grey tea. Get cozy. We pray you will believe us—or at least be entertained.

We see dead people. We hope you don't think we are deranged. We come from good Irish stock. In fact, our grandmother and great-grandmother influenced us greatly as storytellers. We are women creatives of the Irish diaspora, after all. See for yourself.

RORY O'NEILL SCHMITT (RS): HOW DID GREAT-GRANDMA NIX INFLUENCE YOUR STORYTELLING?

ROSARY O'NEILL (RO): Well, I learned storytelling from my her. Grandma (Vera Malter Nix) was glamorous, theatrical, flamboyant. She could silence a room with the squint of her eye, the clench of her jaw.

She was terrified of death and ghosts. Hung a cross on her bedroom door. Would not use the D (devil) word, kept curtains open wide during the day to let in the light. Whenever she got home, she had the chauffeur check under the bed and in the closets for any type of intruder who was going to murder her.

She demanded at least one grandchild be sent to sleep with her in her gargantuan mansion (it was usually me and your Aunt Dale Nix). Every night, she would tell us ghost stories to make us scream and tremble in fear.

We were raised inside her heritage—Catholicism, magical beliefs and superstitions. You and I follow the religious part of her legacy.

RS: HOW DID SHE WARD OFF DEATH?

RO: A superstitious reality controlled her. She protected herself by looking for signs of death. A hat on the bed, a bird in the house, "never two without three."

She was brilliant (a valedictorian, like her mother). But she wouldn't allow thirteen people to sit at table. Because Christ was the thirteenth of the twelve disciples, and he died. She would be screaming if you sat down thirteen at the table.

These beliefs were passed on from her mother, your great-great-grandmother. For instance: If you drop a mirror and it breaks, you're going to die. When her mother was on her deathbed, a mirror fell off the bedstand. She asked, "Did it break?" Grandma said, "No." But she was shaking when she went outside with the splintered glass.

In the Irish tradition, Grandma rejected death by making fun of it. Her best friend's family ran a funeral business. So, naturally, death stalked conversation. She used to say, "Mary, what's the latest in shrouds?"

And Grandma wouldn't live anywhere a person had died. My grandfather built a big new brick mansion on South Carrollton Avenue right after they married. When her cook had a heart attack on the back stairs, he made them drag her outside. He said, "If my wife dies in this house, she's going to make us move."

She would not go to funerals—for fear death was contagious. She only attended her husband's. Anybody else died, she wasn't going to go. Her brother-in-law, her favorite nephew, her-daughter-in law, her only sister? No.

RS: I LOVED LISTENING TO HER GHOST STORIES RECORDING (UNCLE JAY AND AUNT EILEEN RECORDED). CAN YOU TELL US ABOUT THOSE?

RO: Grandma Nix was a great storyteller. Her specialty was ghosts. She told the most awful ghost stories, destined to terrify.[160] We don't know how many of her stories are true or original. (She loved Hans Christian Anderson). She always grounded her stories in the testimony of a devout Irish Catholic priest, beginning them with "Father Daley said…and Father Daley—God rest his soul—would never lie." She told us stories of spirits that seemed improbable. But these had been told to her authentically by people who witnessed them.

RS: WILL YOU SHARE GRANDMA NIX'S GHOST STORY—THE ONE ABOUT THE WIDOW IN HER NEIGHBORHOOD?

RO: Every day, this widow wore a black velvet band on her wrist. Nobody ever could find out why she wore that band. She used to say, "Just before I die, I'll tell you all about it."

After many years, she was growing old and was very sick. She called her children into her room.

She said, "Now, Mother can tell you. I don't think I will live very long. I'm going to tell you the story of my black band on my wrist. Your father never believed in hell. I used to try to make him believe there must be someplace for the dead to go. But I couldn't convince him, he never would listen.

After he died, I woke up one night at 1:00 a.m. I heard the rattle of chains. Smelled smoke. The middle of bedroom just lit up. Then your father appeared walking in chains through the smoke toward the bed. I could hardly see anything but the light on his face and bright light around him.

He said, "Mary, there is a hell, and I'm in it. You don't believe me. I'll leave you a sign, so you'll know." He held up his fingers; they were burning red. He pressed two fingers into my wrist. Left scorch marks on me. I've had to cover them ever since."

Then she removed the velvet band and showed her children the burn marks.

RS: TELL US ABOUT YOUR GHOST ENCOUNTERS. WHEN DID YOU FIRST SEE A GHOST, MAMA? WAS IT AT OUR HOUSE ON CARROLLTON AND JEANNETTE?

RO: I won't go back there, even in my mind. My mother's, grandmother's, great-grandmother's house. Every ghost I ever saw was there. I won't revive memories of so many things that tortured me. Absent presences. Flickering lights. Turning handles. Knocks on the door from nobody. When I stayed there alone, I had to keep all the lights on. Why must we older ones have to recall horrible experiences—just so you have a sense of lineage?

RS: JUST TELL ME ONE GHOST ENCOUNTER, PLEASE? ABOUT THE DEATH VISIT OF THE WOMAN NEXT DOOR.

RO: I don't want to speak about it, lest I call her back. Bald with that urine bag. Or in her fake wig and sequin suit that she folded in her closet inside a plastic box labeled "casket attire." After her death, she blew through my house like a current. Pushing through the front doors. Through the high parlors. Over the sofa where I lay mourning. Out the back door. Down the stairs. The duck in our yard squawked. I rushed to the back door, only to see a hand imprint branding the wood, as if her flesh had been on fire.

RS: LET'S TALK ABOUT HAPPY GHOSTS.

RO: Are there any happy ghosts—really? Bodies decomposing. Souls barred from everything they know and love. Battered and beaten and stabbed. I'm sorry. It's a generational thing. I don't know how this can help you.

RS: YOU'VE GOT TO SHARE ANOTHER ONE OF YOUR GHOST EXPERIENCES.

RO: I was at an artist residency, staying in room number four. I woke up because I felt a presence of someone looking at me. But I didn't *see* anything. I heard dense breathing. I sensed something was floating on the ceiling. I was terrified.

The next morning, I told a staff member about what happened.

She told me, "Yep. That's the suicide room. A woman hanged herself in the bathroom. Somehow, she comes back."

I changed rooms immediately.

RS: DIDN'T YOU CONNECT WITH FAMILY—HOLLY AND BRADLEY—ON THE OTHER SIDE?

RO: Both were killed by fatal mistakes. Holly, thirty-two, because she erroneously put insect strips over her sink. Inhaling poison every day. Dying of stomach cancer. Living on a thread till she birthed her third son.

Bradley, my sweet nephew, squashed by a truck in his backyard. For months, nothing could plug my sister's grief.

One night they both visited me. Holly was with several gloved women by a card table.

"My hands are decomposing," she said. She removed her gloves. Her fingers were stubs. She gestured to Bradley aglow in the field. He was playing with eight boys in the sun.

"They're having a wonderful time," she said.

I was in horror. I've had too many people crossing over tell me how good it was. I don't want to die, even if it's happy over there.

RS: TELL ME ABOUT COUSIN LYNN'S GHOST.

RO: Then will you *be quiet*?

RS: POSSIBLY.

RO: Beloved Cousin Lynn. The pretty one, the one all the boys wanted to marry—with her chiseled features, her long brown hair and blue eyes. She married *up*, a family from political power that owned a compound on the Gulf Coast. She died as swiftly as stomach cancer could take her. We all agonized. Her son became a priest to survive.

RS: WHAT DID SHE TELL YOU IN THAT DREAM?

RO: I saw Lynn on the beach, two children at her side.

She said, "Don't call me back. Don't call me back. I love it here."

"What about your children?" I asked.

She said, "They're fine, don't call me back."

Another dead person telling me they didn't want to come back.

RS: GRANDMA HARTEL VISITED YOU?

RO: Repeatedly at pivotal times in my life. Grandma came to me when I broke up with my now-husband, Bob, and was so devastated. She sat on my bed in that little black and white knit suit she always wore.

She said, "Give him chocolate." She raised her arms. Her arms were like chicken drumsticks.

I tried to get away. I thought: My God, if she comes closer to me, I'm going to die.

I woke up and reached for the light. Slammed over the lamp. Blackness.

Grandma came other times, too. I was struggling to resign from my teaching job. I wanted to write a book on Edgar Degas in New Orleans.

Grandma appeared in a golden chair in front of an apartment in the French Quarter.

I asked her, "Mama, what are you doing here?"

She said, "Write Degas."

I said, "What do you mean: Write Degas?"

The next day, I waited for a final talk with the university president. My eyes darted to a New Orleans artwork by Degas on his wall.

"*The Cotton Office* is my favorite painting," he said.

I thought, "Oh gosh. Here we go."

That's when I resigned as a professor to continue writing about Degas. Good thing I did, because Hurricane Katrina happened the following year. I would've lost my job anyway.

And Grandma visited me at my play reading. Sat in a chair watching. Waiting for me. At first, I didn't recognize her. She looked twenty-eight, the prime age we are supposed to be in the afterlife.

I'm thinking, "Wow, I got to get through this room. Then maybe I won't die today." The dead, I assure you, are waiting for us.

Every night, a ghost-mare seizes me. I'm never ever sleeping without a light. Without a crucifix. Without a rosary in my hand. Without some weapon to ward off evil. If you write or talk or dream about ghosts, they come.

RS: JUST A BIT MORE?

RO: Come on. What about you? When you lived in my house in Queens, you told me you saw a little girl ghost running around.

RS: SHE SAID, "WHY AM I DEAD?"

RO: "Why am I dead?" Absolutely terrified me. I wanted to sell the house immediately.

RS: IT MIGHT'VE BEEN A DREAM. BUT THERE'S MOVEMENT BETWEEN THESE TWO WORLDS: THE DREAM SPACE AND THE REALM OF THE DEAD. MAYBE GHOSTS CAN INTERACT WITH US IN OUR DREAMS.

RO: A point of passage. Certain religions believe that you have the three-day grace to bury someone because the soul of the person can hang around the body. For a while, this point of passage and the dead are still powerful.

RS: GHOSTS CAN WAKE YOU UP AT NIGHT, VISIT YOU IN A DREAM. THEY DON'T EVEN HAVE TO BE A HUMAN FORM OR A PHYSICAL BODY. SOMETIMES, JUST A PRESENCE. A VOICE. A SENSE OF OTHERNESS. ANYTHING ELSE YOU WANT TO ADD?

RO: I believe that the spirit of God lives in us. The most powerful experience I had was the night before my sister died. I had gotten a phone call from her at 10:00 p.m. She said she had Covid, not to worry.

As I walked to my bed, I heard the Holy Spirit speak inside me, "Your sister will die tonight."

It was like…a powerful voice telling me something. It was prescient. I knew it was true. That's how I got through her death. It is what God wanted. If you develop your senses, you can experience a little piece of God.

The next morning, I tried to call Mary, say once, twice, three times.

My brother turned up to my house with his wife. He said, "I've some bad news."

I said, "Mary is dead."

He said, "That's it."

I knew before he said, because I knew God had taken her that night. You have to believe these messages. A lot of people are stupid and don't listen.

Look. Joseph got a vision that he should leave for Egypt. Herod was going to kill all children under the age of two. He didn't say, "Is that really true?" He packed up his stuff and fled with Mary in the middle of the night.

RS: DREAMS ARE LETTERS FROM THE DIVINE.

RO: Exactly. You don't question them. Don't say, "I'm not sure. I'm going to check." No, you need to be willing to hear a dream.

Same thing with Mary. She heard at the Annunciation that she was going to conceive the child. She didn't say, "Where am I going to do it?" She said, "Be it done to me according to thy word."

That's what God wants—a powerful faith. The more faith and hope and goodness you have, the more you will have these experiences. And most of the people who've had visitations or prophetic dreams have had good experiences except the few that have visited hell. But even the scary has been profitable.

RS: I WANT TO MAKE SENSE OF DEATH AND WHAT LIES BEYOND. MAYBE GHOSTS WILL BRING US CLOSER TO GOD.

MORE TERROR

It's easy say ghosts don't exist. But frequent encounters in New Orleans make the paranormal hard to deny.

What kind of city would New Orleans even be without ghosts of our past? So much of our history depends on who went before.

Ghosts manifest in haunted spaces all over the city, reliving events of the past. They're chained to a loop by their trauma. Some say stones record events in history, like the grooves in a record (especially limestone, which is made of old living things). Buildings replay ghostly events under certain circumstances.[161]

Bywater Statue. Photograph by Robert Schaefer Jr.

Ghosts feel at home here in New Orleans. Let's make sense of their encounters with the living. Maybe connecting with the dead will allow us to see a further unfolding of life on different medial planes?[162] Let's stay on the higher planes though. One spiritualist and medium explained:

> *The lower dimensions energetic beings are negative and unfriendly. To survive, they must inspire fear, anxiety, panic, depression. These spirits will manifest into whatever gives you the greatest discomfort for their benefit. If you fear a clown under your bed, that is what will happen.*

Authentic ghost stories contain warning messages. In hushed voices, informants whisper their secret encounters. Read and learn.

ELECTRONICS GOING HAYWIRE

All the electronics in my house went crazy, stereo roared at full blast. I unplugged everything. Then everything went wilder. The radio was emitting the sound of children speaking in tongues. Everything was loud and scary. Things started moving on their own. Flying around the room.

I stayed up all night wide awake. Terrified. I called a friend. He told me, "Get the hell out of there. Bring in a holy person." And that's what I did. The holy person did a blessing, and this bad energy never came back.

Note: As we are finalizing this manuscript, it seems like spirits are interacting with the computer. The cursor randomly jumps down to this section of the book. Highlights the word: *electronics*. This happened five times.

GHOST IMPOSTER

The spirit snarled and yelled, "Get out!"

At that point, I tasted blood in my mouth. It felt like someone was squeezing my cheeks together.

I had to leave this haunted house. If the spirit is demonic, you need a religious leader to help.

I returned with a shaman. When he communicated with the spirit, he learned that the ghost was actually a gentleman who had lived on the property for years. He didn't like the new residents on his property. He was acting demonic to evict them. Get them off his *property.*

GHOST OR DEMON?

I was standing outside of a haunted house with my paranormal investigation team. I heard furniture being thrown inside. But nobody was home. The psychic intuits the spirit inside. She tells us, "This ghost doesn't have a face."

I knew we were in over our heads. I ordered everybody away from the house.

Later, the homeowner admitted, "I forgot to tell you. I was in the laundry room, and something tore the door off the dryer. Threw it across the room."

We were dealing with a demon. If he had told me this, I'd have called a priest…

The difference between a demon and a ghost is that a demon has never been born upon this earth. Demons don't have faces. They don't know how to look human. If a ghost can pick up more than five pounds, it's a demon. Demons are there to scare you, to do you harm.

And in the words of Grandma Nix, "I hope you enjoyed these stories. And that you weren't scared by them. And you won't be kept awake."

ACKNOWLEDGEMENTS

Thanks to God, who gave us the courage to write and joined us as mother and daughter.

We, as a mother-and-daughter team, took hands and went down the road into the unknown. Many people helped us ask bold questions, swim in the unknown and stand face to face with the dead.

Hail to our brilliant editor at The History Press, Joe Gartrell, who encouraged us. We wrote, soaring on the hope you created for us. Knowing an audience was waiting for our book inspired us, as did the always enthusiastic words of senior publicist Jonny Foster. Our happiness was expanded by Katie Parry, Jenni Tyler and Erin Rovin. You made us feel so appreciated, like we were guardians of American history. Well, it is The History Press, and our mission is to celebrate Louisiana's legends.

We salute the artists whose images flood these pages, helping our readers see the worlds we created. Lead photographer Rachelle O'Brien, whose magical pictures and songs lift us into the world of the dead. Stunning photography was provided by Robert Schaefer Jr., Cheryl Gerber and Sam Blankenship. Billy Harris, you helped embed these pages with visual glory.

Informants (whose names have been respectfully omitted for their protection), we thank you for sharing your ghost encounters and trusting us with your innermost thoughts. Special thanks to Mike Huberty and Deanna Duke (American Ghost Walks), Jason Wolf (OPUS network) for their research support.[163]

Mentors, you ignite us with courage: Mark Duplass and Eduardo Machado. You made us believe we could have everything in this world and that it was not unreasonable to expect it if we worked from passion for excellence.

We are grateful to brilliant scholars Dr. C.W. Cannon and Carole DiTosti for their detailed advice.

While we squirreled away, hermetically writing, many trumpeted out song: literary agents Linda Langton and Rachel Swyer; theater agent Tonda Marton and her colleague in Paris, Dominique Christophe; film producer at Serein Productions France and MediaFusion Productions Carole Bidault de L'Isle; New Orleans publicist extraordinaire Heather Harper Cazayoux; our intellectual property Chicago attorney and advisor, Bob Browne; and our brilliant New York producer and attorney, Bill Goodman.

Our hearts fluttered when filmmakers collaborated to make short horror films inspired by this book. Boundless gratitude to producers Melissa Farley and Samantha Bringas. A million thank-yous to the New Orleans "Trapped with Dolls" film team. Thank you to mentor Oley Sassone, who encouraged Rory to direct her first film and guided her graciously along the way. Australian cinematographer Bob Foster painted with light when he composed divine camerawork ("It's just like *Mayfair Witches*, right?" "No. It's better.") Outstanding cast: Kelly Lind, Sherri Eakin and Jeremy Sande (the brilliance, the power, the terror). Tori Bernard, hair and makeup artist extraordinaire. Rachelle O'Brien, tenacious location scout and also an outstanding musician. Rish, thank you for creating the beautiful song, "Sacred Hauntings," with your band partner, the magnificent Eric Laws. Making the music video in the cemetery for the song was unforgettable. (The murder of crows!) Yvonne Lafleur generously provided an elegant wardrobe that made our actresses shine. Gayle Ehrensing (descendant of the Baroness of Pontalba), you graciously opened your stunning home to us. You gifted us magic and *wonder.*

Phoenix team: Ashley Davis (executive director), thank you for welcoming us into the beautiful Rosson House. This Victorian home brought New Orleans to Arizona in "The Elegant Dead." Special thanks also to Shannon Dia (cinematographer) and Iroc Daniels (Glow Frame Initiative) and our amazing crew.

Advocates for the arts, your generosity paves the way for creatives like us: Anne Pincus, Mark Romig and New Orleans & Company, Susan Gore Brennan and Ralph Brennan (our dear cousins and eternal champions of the Napoleon House). Cousin Jay Nix, you never stop believing in us—and even arrive at our book signings with orchids.

Arts patrons, you guided us to achieve the impossible: Anne Jarrell (the Garden District host with the most), Laurie Sapakoff and Evan Cohen; Nell Nolan Young, Bryan Batt, Meg Charbonnet and Lesley Hardin of the National Society of Colonial Dames of America (Louisiana chapter); Lydia Ozenberger, (The Orléans Club); and Hannah House (the Hotel Monteleone). Our gratitude to Jennifer Weidinger, whose friendship has inspired and comforted us in New Orleans, San Diego, Los Angeles, Scottsdale, and Gothenberg.

Additional supporters, we salute Jerry Daigle, Frank Hart, Nell Nolan Young, Lt. Governor Billy Nungesser, Villa Albertine, CODOFIL, New Orleans and Company, and Women in Film & TV Louisiana.

Fellow writers, historians, journalists and book lovers, you graciously shared our stories: Jeanne Nathan (*Crosstown Conversations*, radio), Susan Larson (*The Reading Life*, NPR), Megan Meehan and Carroll Gelderman at her unforgettable Garden District Book Shop.

To France, *nous vous remercions*: Rodolphe Sambou (Consulate General of France in Louisiana), Jacques Baran (cultural attaché of France to New Orleans) and Gabi Grenier (cultural program officer, Consulate General of France in Louisiana). Your glamorous reception at the consulate's residence in the Garden District is a memory we will never forget. *Merci mille fois* to our sister city, Paris: Michèle Puyserver (France–Louisiane Association board member), Annick Foucrier (professor emerita, The Sorbonne), Amélie Gonin (Foyer International d'Accueil de Paris–Jean Monnet), Genevieve Acker, Martine Roussel (executive director, Fulbright Commission, Paris) and Pierre de Pontalba (fourth-great-grandson of the Baroness of Pontalba).

To the Motherland, Ireland, we toast with gratitude. *Go raibh maith agat*! Robbie Hull (Consul General of Ireland, Austin, representing Louisiana, Texas, Missouri, Oklahoma, Kansas and Arkansas) and Cecilia Tirado (community and culture officer at the Department of Foreign Affairs and Trade, Ireland in Austin). We strive to honor St. Brigid and her women creatives of the Irish diaspora. After all, the holy remains at the heart of it all. At the Consulate General of Ireland in Los Angeles, we wish to thank Marcella Smyth (Consul General of Ireland in Los Angeles, representing Arizona, Hawaii, Nevada, New Mexico, Southern California and Utah) and Siobhán Quinlan (head of cultural affairs at the Consulate General of Ireland in Los Angeles). At the magical Tyrone Guthrie Centre, we thank Anna Walsh (director) and the family of Irish artists we met at the residency in Annaghmakerrig: Melissa O'Donnell, Louise Neiland and

Tyrone Guthrie Centre, Annaghmakerrig House, Ireland. *Photograph by Rory O'Neill Schmitt, PhD.*

Hugh Hick. Newbliss is truly bliss. To our Irish compatriots in Paris, we are grateful to Hugh Farrell (head of cultural affairs, Embassy of Ireland, Paris); Niall Burgess (ambassador of Ireland to France); Nora Hickey M'Sichili (director of the Irish Cultural Center in Paris); Father Jim Doyle, Loretto Mara, Donal O'Neill and Eugene Brennan (friends at the Irish Cultural Center, Paris); and Paul Howard (Dublin filmmaker of *Infinite Potential*).

We are forever grateful to our ancestors on both sides. I (Rory) prayed to my Irish ancestors for strength while I wrote this book in Ireland. And I heard, "You are a writer. You are a writer. You are a writer." Thank you for giving us faith to keep going.

Brilliant and beautiful friends fueled our passion as we wrote: Laura Ferlin, Dr. Katie Keresit, Allison Lee, Clair Brown, Lauren Wincott, Jill Boatright, Ray Fitz and Dr. Erin Wibbins. From California to Louisiana to New York, you showered us with your support: David and Rexanne Becnel, George Trahanis, Jim Bosjolie, Brownie Fitzpatrick, Rachel Friend and Karen Engleman. Your courage and artistry encourage us: Mary Koppel (Episcopalian priest and writer), Susan Izatt (New York City director), David Hurland (Marigny Opera House founder) and Sally

Nola Angel, St. Louis Cemetery No. 3. Photograph by Rachelle O'Brien.

Ann Glassman (Vodou priestess). Thank you for always showing up, picking up, lifting us up.

University of Southern California colleagues, you filled our hearts with Trojan courage: Dr. Melinda Thomas, Monica Keyes, Will Terry, Dr. Jennifer Hawe, Jessica Golden, Alexis Hackathorn, Liz Phillips, Jayda Imlahen and Dr. John Keim. USC faculty, you inspired us to reach for the stars, especially Dr. Carly Cooper, who cheered us to the finish line. USC Staff Assembly officers, Stacey Croomes, Stacy Patterson and Phillip Turner, and executive committee and members, you inspire the entire USC community.

As a mother-daughter team, we completed this book venture buttressed by our family's love: Bob Harzinski, Dr. Dasan Schmitt and Olivia and Rowan Schmitt; Dr. Dale Ellen O'Neill, Tim, Wyatt and Colette Springer; and Rachelle, Scott, Ruby, Cooper Geerds, Barret, Miranda and Avelyn O'Brien.

What curative can soothe the terrified? *Art. Story. Film.* Barret O'Brien creates enchanting poetry that resonates with the spirit-filled city of New Orleans. His mystic words shimmer and magnetize the world. We salute Barret O'Brien and all artists, writers, filmmakers and dreamers from Louisiana.

Louisiana family, thank you for always welcoming us home: Stephen and Pat Hartel, Joe and Jean Hartel, Eileen and Dale Nix.

My (Rory) gratitude goes to my Irish father, Richard Patrick O'Neill. Papa O. tells the best ghost stories (some of which are included in this book).

Arizona family and friends, your joy boosts our lives, especially during Sunday Family Home Evenings: Vicki and Brett Schmitt, Jasmine Stevenson, Maya Schmitt, Casey Franklin, Betsy Franklin, Lauryn Bymers, Tanya Henry, Corey Allor, Gina Saunders, Naya Aboujaoude and Emiy Fager.

To our forever friend, Dawn Henry: please keep visiting us in our dreams. *My life's so much easier now. My life's so much easier now. My life's so much easier now.*

We will never forget our ancestors who paved the way: Vera Nix, James T. Nix, Jacob Malter, Rosary Nix Hartel, Stephen Hartel, Mary Hartel Anderson, Joseph O'Neill, Dorothy Donovan O'Neill, Elsie O'Neill, Marguerite Schmitt and Candy Schmitt Martinez. May you fly with angels' wings.

Thank you to our forever home, our *muse*, our first love: New Orleans.

Most glorious, praise to God and the saints of compassion, who keep us writers poised to envision, imagine and create.

With love from New Orleans, Louisiana; Scottsdale, Arizona; Paris, France; and Dublin, Ireland.
Rosary O'Neill, PhD and Rory O'Neill Schmitt, PhD

NOTES

Forward Through Fear

1. "Mezzo del cammin di nostra vita." Dante Alighieri, *Inferno*, vol. 1 (1321), 1.
2. A tool for protection in New Orleans Voodoo.

Chapter 1

3. As fire broke out on Good Friday 1788, Father Antoine refused to allow the church bells to ring in warning, a decision that would lead to the destruction of most of the city and its beloved church.
4. The Cabildo historic building once housed a prison (calabozo).
5. Extremist forays, like the Battle of the Cabildo, exploded during the nineteenth century. The Cabildo housed a prison yard. In front of the Cabildo, horrific public executions were performed before crowds of onlookers. Locals watched public hangings during family outings and social gatherings on Jackson Square. A New Orleans historian shared with us: "The area in front of the Cabildo was one of the first social areas. City organizers wanted to make a place where locals could have social gatherings, a place where families could go for outings. The military barracks were next to the Cabildo, and prisoners were held there. Outside the Cabildo, there would be public hangings. People would watch these executions on family outings. That was the regular outdoor fun back then: executions for the prisoners."
6. He shared his ghost spottings with investigators in a documentary film. We reached out him to discover more about his experiences, but he is nowhere to be found.

7. The BK (short for the general and the authoress who owned the house) House is located at on 1113 Chartres Street.
8. The Giacona family purchased the BK House in 1904. Corrado Giacona (1875–1944) was the first boss of the New Orleans crime family. Some surmise it's the ghost of the New Orleans mafia boss reliving his violent past, shooting four men on the back gallery.
9. Louisiana historian Joe Gray Taylor dubbed Beauregard the "Napoleon in gray."
10. A judge once inhabited this house with his wife, nine children and extended family.
11. The scent of roses has been associated with sanctity in Catholic traditions.
12. An entry table beckons you with calling cards and Mrs. Grima's death announcement from October 15, 1850.

Chapter 2

13. 1140 Royal Street
14. Refer to George Washington Cable, *Strange True Stories of Louisiana* (Arcadia Publishing, 1994); Herbert Asbury, *French Quarter: An Informal History of the New Orleans Underworld* (Basic Books, 2003).
15. Some say the crowd that gathered included four thousand local residents.
16. Madame LaLaurie fled to Paris and avoided facing the consequences. She died in Paris but had arranged for herself to be reinterred in New Orleans in 1851. There, she gloats and decays, lording over St. Louis Cemetery No. 1, not far from her house of terror.
17. Homeless youth experience psychosomatic paralysis outside of Madame LaLaurie's house. Interview with Rachelle O'Brien, New Orleanian, September 26, 2024.
18. Invisible spirits physically assaulted young girls (who later went to a school there).
19. Carolyn Morrow Long, *Madame Lalaurie, Mistress of the Haunted House* (University Press of Florida, 2012).
20. US Ghost Adventures purchased Madame LaLaurie's mansion in October 2024.
21. Some leading paranormal researchers point to New Orleans's vicious history of slavery and the slave trade. One spiritualist we met with shared that New Orleans is a city where slavery is ingrained. The history of oppression that occurred on the land is a reason why the city is so haunted. She shared with us a ghost experience she had: "A woman ghost took my spirit out of my body, flew my astral body above New Orleans, over Bourbon Street. She told me, 'This is our city.' I looked down at it, and I saw a negative, dark energy pattern." Interview, October 1, 2024.
22. Interview with Pierre de Pontalba, fourth-great-grandson of the Baroness de Pontalba, November 6, 2024.
23. A decade passed, and Micaela, now titled the Baroness of Pontalba (as her husband became the baron) was restituted some of her property by a Louisiana judge. She stood up for her own rights, fought inheritance, government and property law, and triumphed over a wicked father-in-law, who pursued her for

years trying to get her money. The baroness protected herself with her iron-fisted will. Interview with Gayle Ehrensing, New Orleanian descendant of the Baroness of Pontalba, October 7, 2024.

24. Micaela returned to New Orleans with her two sons during the outbreak of the French Revolution. She integrated into fashionable society, where she was seen as a vivacious, intelligent and business-like woman. Once she noticed that the French Quarter was becoming run-down and derelict, she decided to make a change for the better. She demolished her buildings next to St. Louis Cathedral and oversaw the construction of the famous Pontalba properties (1848–51).
25. According to a paranormal historian in New Orleans, two ghosts haunt the lower side of the building (on Jackson Square), and one lingers on the upper side. Interview with Deanna X, American Ghost Walks guide, New Orleans, September 10, 2024.
26. Dr. Dupas lived in this location from 1855 to 1867.
27. Did this pharmacist dip tampons in opium and belladonna to treat menstrual cramps?

Chapter 3

28. Interview with Jason Wolf, OPUS network, November 19, 2024.
29. New Orleans is a necropolis, which is a cemetery belonging to an ancient city.
30. Interview with Dr. Charles Cannon, a New Orleans scholar, 2024.
31. St. Louis No. 1 is located at 425 Basin Street. Basin Street was known for its blues, jazz and red-light meetups.
32. Mark Twain called places like this "cities of the dead" because the dead are buried in marble vaults aboveground. Run down a path here between these houses and temples and then squint at the roofs and gables. Indeed, the cemetery looks like a city.
33. 2300 North Claiborne Avenue
34. St. Louis No. 2 once ran from Canal Street to St. Louis Street. For the construction of the expressway, five hundred homes and businesses were vanquished.
35. The New Orleans Cemetery Preservation Society is determined to save historical markers like these. The Louisiana Landamarks Society is another notable non-profit preserving historic architecture in New Orleans.
36. Save Our Cemeteries, a wonderful charity, is trying to fight for and restore St. Louis No. 2. Sponsors fight off the destruction of the tomb walls and replacement with metal fencing. Yellow fever has ravaged the population of New Orleans during the city's founding in 1718 and on and off through the 1800s.
37. St Louis No. 1 was unharmed by the freeway.
38. In 1820, the City Council insisted on locating a new cemetery at least 2,400 feet from the city limits; the nearest practical site, on what is now Claiborne Avenue, was only 1,800 feet from Rampart Street. It was consecrated in 1823.

39. Kathryn Olivarius, "New Outbreak, Familiar Anxieties: Stanford Historian Examines Yellow Fever Outbreak in 19th-Century New Orleans," Stanford University, March 25, 2020.
40. This period in the nineteenth century included the Louisiana Purchase and the Civil War. Epidemics killed thousands in New Orleans during the summer. Many locals fled New Orleans in the summertime and were treated to the country, like the Mississippi Gulf Coast.
41. Alligators are most common in Louisiana's coastal marshes, but they can be found in ponds, lakes, canals, rivers, swamps, and bayous. Although alligator attacks in Louisiana are rare, they do happen.
42. Gothic script was prevalent in western Europe from the 1100s to the 1600s. and used much longer in Germany, throughout the nineteenth and until the twentieth century.
43. Anne Rice's house in New Orleans's Garden District is located at 1239 First Street. The Greek Revival–style house with Italianate elements was purchased by Rice in 1989 and was her home until 2004. Rice wrote her trilogy *The Lives of the Mayfair Witches* while living there, and the books are set there.
44. Anne Rice's *The Witching Hour* and *Interview with a Vampire* contain fictional characters buried in Lafayette Cemetery No. 1 in New Orleans, Louisiana. The Mayfair Witches of *The Witching Hour* and *Interview with the Vampire*'s crypts were modeled from the Jefferson fireman tomb and the Karstendiek family tomb, respectively. The Karstendiek family tomb, a "customized" cast-iron structure, is better known as "Lestat's Tomb," thanks to author Anne Rice. Peter B. Deder, *The Cemeteries of New Orleans: A Cultural History*, 1st ed. (Louisiana State University Press, 2017). While promoting her 1995 novel *Memnoch the Devil*, author Anne Rice emerged from a coffin after riding through the cemetery. Lafayette was the city's first planned cemetery, and she was the queen of the darkness. The cemetery was named after the city of Lafayette, which was once located in the area of New Orleans. Established in 1833, with almost five hundred wall vaults, this nondenominational cemetery has a rich history with the resting places of some of the city's first settlers from Ireland and Germany.
45. Located at 1400 Washington Avenue.
46. Visitors can get lost meandering through this century-old gravesite.
47. Of the forty-two cemeteries in the New Orleans metro area, Metairie Cemetery is considered the most beautiful and elaborate. With structured tombs, abandoned British castles and grandiose mausoleums, it's no wonder that this historic cemetery was listed as a National Historic Landmark in 1991.
48. Anne Rice's husband and her wee daughter are buried alongside her.
49. Cemetery workers have seen this ghost leaving her post at night to stroll among the tombs.
50. The cemetery was opened here in 1872, while many businesses were going bankrupt. Bereft men dueled to the death at the Dueling Oaks or hanged

themselves in City Park, not far from here. Painter Edgar Degas, in 1872, visited to try to save his uncle's cotton business.

Chapter 4

51. Commander's Palace was built in 1880 by Emile Commander. He brought the restaurant to international popularity by 1900. Chef Commander died from tuberculosis at the age of forty-eight and was buried in Metairie Cemetery.
52. For more information on gambling, see Troy Taylor, *Wicked New Orleans: The Dark Side of the Big Easy* (The History Press, 2010). Napoleonic law allowed Pierre Jourdain's wife to inherit the property.
53. Rex is the carnival krewe that puts on the leading parade of Mardi Gras Day. See O'Neill, *New Orleans Carnival Krewes* (The History Press, 2014).
54. Antoine's is in a cluster of buildings fronting St. Louis Street. The front entrance opens into the Main Dining Room, which was the original restaurant. Inside that room and to the left is the largest dining room, The Annex. A series of small dining rooms are entered from The Annex toward the Bourbon Street side: The Dungeon, The 1840 Room, The Proteus Room and The Escargot Room. Directly behind The Annex and across a hall from The Proteus Room is The Rex Room.
55. Other hauntings at Antoine's include lights being illuminated at odd times in offices that were left dark and locked.
56. Antoine's is just another restaurant where founder owners haunt: Commander's (Emil Commander), Muriel's (Pierre Antoine Lepardi Jourdan) and Tujaque's (Julian Eltinge).
57. Located on the corner of Bourbon and St. Philip Streets, the shop was used as a base for the smuggling operations of Jean Lafitte and his brother Pierre.
58. Pirates, on average, died in their mid-thirties due to their many occupational hazards. Medical complications abounded: scurvy, mosquito-borne diseases, infectious diseases and gangrene. Some say pirates lasted in their chosen career for only two years before they died.
59. Jean Lafitte was born in 1780 and died in 1823. Lafitte became a local legend during the War of 1812 when he helped Andrew Jackson defend the city of New Orleans from capture at the hands of the British. Following the war, Lafitte received a pardon from President James Madison for his service and resumed his career as a pirate on Galveston's Island in Spanish Texas. Lafitte had five children and later became a widower when his wife died after the birth of his third daughter. He then had a public relationship with a free woman of color and fathered two more children.
60. Refer to our book *New Orleans Voodoo: A Cultural History*.

Chapter 5

61. Vodou is a religion practiced in Haiti. Some Voodoo priests and priestesses we know in New Orleans have been initiated in Haiti.
62. We learned that lwas are intermediaries for God. These spirits are often syncretized as Catholic saints. For example, St. Barbara, the patron saint of warriors, is also recognized as Shango, the African Vodun god of war. Shango teaches believers how to "pull our power down from the heavens," says local priestess Janet Evans. Many enslaved laborers prayed to Shango. Voodoo is powerful and invites an authentic sense of agency. In Louisiana's history, openly practicing Voodoo was prohibited.
63. Believers combine, mold and integrate traditions in New Orleans Voodoo.
64. For more information, refer to *New Orleans Voodoo: A Cultural History* (The History Press, 2018) by Rory Schmitt, PhD and Rosary O'Neill, PhD.
65. The Voodoo Museum exhibits chromolithographs, photography, paintings, skeletons and drapos (sequined tapestries).
66. Voodoo Authentica of New Orleans Cultural Center and Collection's owner, Brandi Kelly, is a Haiti-initiated Vodou priestess. She is the founder of the original Voodoo Fest, which includes music, educational events and celebration for the New Orleans community every year.
67. Visit the comforting mystic here, Vodou priestess Sallie Ann Glassman. Sallie Ann was initiated in Vodou in Haiti. For an explanation of the differences between New Orleans Voodoo and Vodou, refer to our *New Orleans Voodoo: A Cultural History.*
68. See our interview with Sallie Ann Glassman in *New Orleans Voodoo: A Cultural History.*
69. Voodoo encourages empowerment and agency.
70. The sculpture was created by artist Ricardo Pustanio.
71. Snakes in Voodoo often refer to Damballa, the sky-serpent lwa.
72. In 1821, Marie Laveau partnered with Captain Christophe Glapion, an aristocrat in New Orleans. Interracial marriages were illegal in Louisiana. Laveau and Glapion lived together for thirty-four years in their home at 15 St. Ann Street.
73. Interview with Erin X, New Orleanian and Voodoo practitioner, ghost witness, August 11, 2024.
74. In Congo Square, Marie Laveau danced with a snake called La Grande Zombie, which means "undead person" in Haiti.
75. Interview with Allison X, July 3, 2024.
76. Many perceived the younger as the elder Marie Laveau and confused the two, assuming immortality and otherworldly powers. Both now lie in the Glapion family tomb in St. Louis No. 1. However, some claim the younger's body was moved to St. Louis No. 2 and say that she remains in a wall vault here. For additional information on Marie Laveau, refer to *The Spirited Lives of Marie Laveau* (University Press of Mississippi, 2004). Refer to Schmitt and O'Neill, *A Cultural History of Voodoo.*
77. Interview with Alayha X, energy worker, July 11, 2024.
78. Interview with Charlotte K.

79. Interview with Allison X, Christian youth leader, July 3, 2024.
80. Our friend Charlotte Kossa, the host of *California Haunts Radio*, leads a paranormal investigation team.
81. One Magick practitioner from New Orleans told us that some practitioners can shut down spiritual vortexes. They purposely create sacred spaces for a short period. Then they can move the negative spirits there. Banish them. Some spiritual leaders perform exorcisms of buildings. Interview with Tennie X, psychic medium and spiritualist clergy member for over forty years, August 16, 2024.
82. Interview with Charlotte Kossa, paranormal investigator, *California Haunts Radio* podcaster, July 12, 2024.
83. Our Episcopal priest distinguished home blessings from exorcisms. Interview with Mary X, Episcopalian priest, October 14, 2024.

Chapter 6

84. Henriette de Lisle's mother was a woman of color; her French father was Anglo.
85. Henriette de Lisle said, "Je crois en Dieu. J'espère en Dieu. Je veux vivre et mourir pour Dieu." ("I believe in God. I hope in God. I want to live and die for God.")
86. During documentation of the beatification process for DeLille, the congregation found funeral records from the 1820s that suggested, as a teenager, she gave birth to two sons. Both children (named Henry Bocno) died at a young age.
87. Henriette is in the second step of the process of being declared a saint by the Catholic Church.
88. The first healing, that of a four-year-old child whose life was threatened by double pneumonia and a severe bacterial infection, occurred in the 1990s. The second healing occurred in 2007 after a young college student suffered a brain aneurism and slipped into a coma.
89. Tombs can hold from sixty to one hundred people and operate as slow-working furnaces.
90. Henriette de Lisle is buried in the same tomb as her Sisters of the Holy Family cofounders, Juliette Gaudin and Josephine Charles. In 1988, Pope John Paul II declared de Lisle a servant of God, beginning her canonization process for sainthood. The Sisters of the Holy Family still serve New Orleans. They teach, nurse the poor and elderly and maintain vigils at the bedsides of the dying. While other orders' numbers have declined, the Sisters of the Holy Family have multiplied from just twelve when Henriette died to over ninety-six in New Orleans today. They have diverse missions throughout Louisiana; Texas; California; Washington, D.C.; and Belize.
91. Charity Hospital was destroyed in Hurricane Katrina and is supposedly in the process of being rebuilt.

92. New Orleans' location, population growth (1820–60) and poor sanitation made it a prime target for these diseases. The city's low elevation, high water table and location between Lake Pontchartrain and the Mississippi River made it difficult to drain, and clean water was hard to come by.
93. Officials also learned that additional miracles had been attributed to Elizabeth's intercession with God: a child was miraculously cured of leukemia, and a man recovered miraculously from a massive brain infection.
94. The patient had been diagnosed with a very aggressive terminal cancer when they initially performed surgery. A few months later, she appeared to be recovering. Dr. Nix performed an exploratory surgery and found no evidence of any cancer cells remaining in her entire body. Shortly before he died in 1945, Grandfather Nix testified to some Vatican representatives who came to New Orleans to take his testimony about a miracle that was later related to a canonization. Our grandmother/great-grandmother Nix said that they had a hospital bed in her library. Grandfather Nix was very weak with heart problems at the time. She said that they installed Swiss Guards at the double doors that connected the library to the living room to ensure privacy and confidentiality for their inquiry. The recovery was determined to be a miracle for Saint Elizabeth Seton. Shortly before he died in 1945, Grandfather Nix testified to some Vatican representatives who came to New Orleans to take his testimony about a miracle that was later related to a canonization.
95. Prominent places in New Orleans salute this spirit's goodness, like the Saint Martin de Porres Center for campus ministry at the University of New Orleans and the St. Martin de Porres Chapel at Tulane University. This chapel was sponsored by Gail and Tom Benson and was dedicated in 2019 on Tulane University's campus. At the dedication, the chaplain shared, "St. Martin de Porres, a great apostle of charity and patron of social justice who, despite suffering greatly because of his mixed race, set a profound example of love of God and neighbor."
96. Pope John XXXIII canonized Saint Martin in 1962. Saint Martin de Porres (1579–1639) is the patron saint of social justice, harmony and mixed-race peoples.
97. In Peru, Martin de Porres cured the sick, and during his lifetime, people even started to call him a saint. He was known for communicating with animals. He lived a life of almost constant prayer, practiced unbelievable austerities and worked on hard and menial tasks without ever losing a moment of union with God.
98. St. Martin was sighted in Mexico, Central America and Japan by people who knew him well. But he never left Lima after he entered the Order. Some say he even passed through locked doors. Others reported he appeared at the bedside of sufferers without being asked. He also soothed the sick, even when he did not completely cure them. Even sick animals came to him for healing.
99. The Old Ursuline Convent was erected in 1745.
100. This chapel facing Ursulines Street was dedicated on March 19, 1787. The chapel had been named Our Lady of Victory.

101. This wooden statue, painted gold, was carved in France. Visitors can still see this statue during daily mass at the Ursuline Chapel, located off Claiborne Avenue in New Orleans.
102. He's a controversial saint.
103. St. Jude was one of Christ's original apostles and a cousin of Jesus. St. Jude died in 65 BCE. The relic of his arm is the oldest relic of a saint.
104. The Shrine of Our Lady of Guadalupe hosted the forearm of St. Jude, which is considered a first-class relic.
105. St. Anna Church is located on Esplanade Avenue. This is the third church built for St. Anna's since 1846.

Chapter 7

106. We learned about the theory of the thin veil between worlds in Ireland from a colleague at the Tyrone Guthrie Centre. This part belief is part of ancient Celtic tradition.
107. New Orleans has a vicious history of oppression. New Orleans is both the light and the dark of spiritual energy. Some leading paranormal researchers point to the tragedy and oppression that occurred in New Orleans as the reason it's now a hotbed for ghosts. Interview with a psychic and spiritualist medium, 2024.
108. The 1967 movie *Hotel*, starring Karl Malden, was filmed at the Hotel Monteleone.
109. In 1998, the American Library Association made the Hotel Monteleone a literary landmark. William Faulkner wrote *The Sound and the Fury* and Tennessee Williams wrote *The Rose Tattoo* there.
110. Strangely, she watches with rapt attention, the expression on her face serene.
111. Wounded soldiers were treated with heinously provincial medicine.
112. This ballroom has seen many events—weddings in the present day and theatrical performances in the 1990s (including Southern Rep, founded by Rosary).
113. Quadroon balls referred to the mixed-race women of color who attended these events. They were then referred to as quadroons, or people who were one-fourth Black.
114. From 1792 to 1794, this location served as an orphanage and a boardinghouse.
115. Spain controlled New Orleans from 1762 until 1803, when the Louisiana Territory was ceded back to France. Essentially, Spanish rule over New Orleans lasted for nearly forty years.
116. Five boys haunt rooms 107 and 109. A strange, eerie feeling poisons the air, as though someone—or something—is watching. Lights and faucets flick off and on.
117. Armond reappears in room 208.
118. In 2016, the investigators recorded their experience—an experience we deem to be true. The ghost hunter's wooden cross snapped in half in his hand. A peculiar voice of a little boy rang out. Invisible children laughed. The ghost children told him, "We are hiding."

119. The ghost of a caretaker also patrols. Her disembodied footsteps climb the stairs day and night. She obsessively straightens up, plumping pillows, shoving back furniture. She probably knows what happened to the five ghost boys.
120. General Andrew Jackson, shortly after his victory over the British in the Battle of New Orleans, was held in contempt of court there. Many guests have claimed they spotted his ghost parading around the halls of the hotel.
121. Built in 1833, the house had various residents before it became a brothel. A movement to sweep the area of crime in the late 1860s dispersed brothels farther into the Vieux Carre. Hotel Villa Convento was built in the 1830s and started out as a plot of land owned by the Ursuline nuns, who sold it to Jean Baptiste Poeyfarre. He built a creole townhouse, which changed hands and became a brothel after the Civil War. The brothel catered to all manner of folk who arrived by land and sea. They needed a house of ill repute, where they could drink, gamble and more. Jimmy Buffet was a short termer in room 305 during the early years of his career. What ghosts did he encounter? He sings, "Vampires, mummies, and the Holy Ghost," words that terrify.
122. From the song "House of the Rising Sun." The lyrics are in the public domain, as it is a traditional folk song with an unknown original author, meaning no one holds a copyright to the song itself.
123. Eric Burdon was a musician resident who composed music here.
124. There are different versions of this song, one from a male perspective and one from a woman's (a sex worker's). The male's point of view was recorded by musicians, including Roy Acuff in the 1930s and others in the 1920s and 1930s, though the folk song is likely much older.
125. The child ghost in room 302 may be less threatening. She could actually be eight or nine.
126. This was the time of brothels and houses of assignation in Storyville in New Orleans (1897–1917).
127. This exquisite Uptown mansion was built in 1883 and has been a hotel since 1953.
128. Louis Malle's controversial 1978 Storyville movie. The interior of the brothel in that film is the Columns Hotel.
129. By 1883, Simon Hersheim and his family had moved into the Columns Hotel building.

Chapter 8

130. Anne Rice was part of the Irish diaspora and was raised in the Irish Channel District in New Orleans.
131. Anne was sober for years. Her childhood trauma influenced her to make sure her son wasn't raised by a parent with alcoholism. Anne's mother, who died of alcoholism, told Anne her addiction was a craving in her blood. We knew Anne Rice. Her son studied acting at our theater, Southern Rep. We honored both Anne and Christopher at our fundraiser at Antoine's Restaurant. Only

he appeared. Every year, she donated a slew of signed books to the fundraiser. The house, 1239 First Street in New Orleans, also known as the Brevard-Clapp House or the Rosegate Home, is a Greek Revival–Italianate mansion built in 1857. It was the setting for many of Rice's books, including her Mayfair Witches trilogy.

132. Her research of how to get blood for her dying five-year-old led Anne to write her first vampire book, *Interview with the Vampire.*

133. Lafayette No. 1 isn't far from the mansion of the Consul General of France and the chic private girls' school, McGees.

134. According to New Orleans folklore, "Vampire Jacques," also known as Jacques Saint-Germain or the Count of Saint Germain, is said to have lived in New Orleans. A mysterious figure, he may have been alive for centuries, potentially back to the time of Christ.

135. Rory is the nickname for Rosary, combining the first two and last two letters of her name.

136. The Mayfair Witches from Anne Rice's *The Witching Hour* and *Interview with the Vampire* are fictional characters buried in Lafayette Cemetery No. 1 in New Orleans, Louisiana. Rice's depiction of the Mayfair Witches' tomb is based on a combination of the Lafayette and Jefferson fireman tombs and the Karstendiek family tomb in the cemetery. The Karstendiek family tomb, a "customized" cast-iron structure, is better known as "Lestat's Tomb," thanks to author Anne Rice. See Peter Deder, *The Cemeteries of New Orleans: A Cultural History* (Louisiana State University Press, 2017).

137. Quotes from Anne Rice's husband's poems and writings and an entire wall of stained glass span the walls.

Chapter 9

138. Uptown refers to a location in the city in relation to the flow of the Mississippi River.

139. Refer to Veenu Sandal, "The Lesser-Known World of Water Spirits," *The Sunday Guardian*, August 25, 2018, https://sundayguardianlive.com/opinion/lesser-known-world-water-spirits.

140. The area around Audubon Park in New Orleans, Louisiana, is called Audubon, a neighborhood in the Uptown/Carrollton area. It's also known as the University District because it's home to Tulane and Loyola Universities.

141. Audubon Park is a municipal park located in the Uptown neighborhood of New Orleans. It comprises approximately 350 acres. The site of Audubon Park was once bought and owned by Pierre Foucher. Foucher fled to France before the Civil War.

142. These are called shotgun houses because a bullet fired through their front door would go right out the back door without hitting a wall.

143. Camelbacks are narrow houses (because taxes were once levied on a house's width) with a hump or raised unit in the back.
144. The Garden District in New Orleans has both police and private security patrols.
145. Their bright green plumage makes them difficult to spot among the palm tree fronds.
146. Not too far away is the convent of the Academy of the Sacred Heart, where German shepherds used to be let free on the grounds to protect the Carmelite nuns at night.
147. The old U.S. Mint anchors the avenue at the other end.
148. In the 1830s, Esplanade was extended in segments from the river's edge through a succession of habitations, or plantations, to Bayou Saint John. It was a residential "garden suburb" for the city's Francophone elite. A *Times-Picayune* article from 1852 describes it as "the handsomest street in the city… with a broad space in the center planted with a double row of forest trees, now forming a long arch of bright, thick verdure to shade the grass below."
149. New Orleans had the largest slave market in America, and the French Quarter Riverfront was the center of activity. Some believe New Orleans is brimming with ghosts. They stem from the city's history of slavery and institutionalized racism.
150. Estelle's family lived in several New Orleans houses, each one smaller than the one before. From a Garden District mansion they owned, Estelle moved to a two-story rental house on Esplanade, 2918 Esplanade Avenue, to a sad two-bedroom cottage on Bayou Saint John.
151. Estelle Musson Degas was also Edgar and Rene Degas's first cousin—intermarriage was quite common back then. Edgar Degas's mother, Celestine Musson, was born in New Orleans, and her family had resided in Louisiana for generations.
152. René Degas abandoned Estelle and his American children. He married his next-door neighbor, and they fled New Orleans and moved to France. Because of René's betrayal, Edgar did not speak to him for ten years.
153. The Buchner House is located at 1410 Jackson Avenue.
154. The first owners, dead from yellow fever and a lightning strike, probably won't appear.
155. This ghost is reportedly their niece who drowned in a lake nearby.
156. Certain types of greenery, particularly large trees, are often associated with attracting ghosts or spirits.
157. The Dueling Oak is located at 29591 Dreyfous Drive.
158. Edgar Degas's uncle indeed challenged someone to a duel in the late 1800s.

Experts and Authors Reflect on America's Most Haunted City

159. Mother-daughter interview, Rory Schmitt interviews Rosary O'Neill, July 1, 2024.
160. Grandmother Nix, Tales of Terror, a recording of ghost and scary stories, New Orleans, date unknown.

More Terror

161. This theory comes from a 1972 BBC movie called *The Stone Tape*. An interview with Mike Huberty, America Ghost Walks founder, August 8, 2024.
162. Interview with Jason Wolf, OPUS network, November 19, 2024.

Acknowledgements

163. We partnered with the Organization for Paranormal Understanding and Support nonprofit for our research. They distributed our survey about ghosts to their network of over four thousand members. We received several survey responses. Findings from this small sample aligned with existing scholarship in the fields of psychology, sociology, cultural studies and parapsychology. Our discoveries included: Certain locations were more likely to host ghostly presences due to their historical or emotional significance. Common haunted locations are graveyards, battlefields, hospitals, churches and historical buildings. Ghosts have physical and mental impacts. Ghosts appear in various forms, from human-like figures to ambiguous shapes. They exhibit a range of behaviors, from standing still to interacting physically, moving objects. Ghosts can be guides or teachers. One anonymous survey participant wrote, "Ghosts just want to communicate—usually."

ABOUT THE AUTHORS

Photograph by Traci Bower.

RORY O'NEILL SCHMITT, PHD, is a visiting Fulbright Scholar (2024–27), specializing in visual art and education. She leads faculty development at University of Southern California and serves as vice president of USC Staff Assembly.

Dr. Schmitt has authored five books, published by The History Press, including *Navajo and Hopi Art in Arizona* (2016). She has coauthored with Dr. Rosary O'Neill *New Orleans Voodoo: A Cultural History* (2019), *Edgar Degas in New Orleans* (2023), *Kate Chopin in New Orleans* (2024) and *The Haunted Guide to New Orleans* (2025). Her poem, "Naked Mermaid Talks to God," was a finalist in the Faulkner Society Wisdom Creative Writing Competition (2024).

A filmmaker, she produced the Duplass Brothers Productions television series *A Long Long Night*, costarring Mark Duplass and Barret O'Brien, which premiered at Tribeca Festival, was screened at South by Southwest and is currently streaming on Kinema. Rory moderated the panel "The Future of Indie Film" with Bruce Campbell at the Ashland Independent Film Festival. She produced the short film *Garden District* (written by Rosary O'Neill), which was heralded globally for best film, best director and best actors.

For her books and films, she has been honored by the French Consulate of New Orleans and the Consul General of Ireland in Austin. She has been invited to artist residencies at the Tyrone Guthrie Centre (Annaghmakerrig, Ireland) and the Irish Cultural Center (Paris). She has led lectures and presentations at the New Orleans Museum of Fine Art, Pitot House, Foyer International d'Accueil Paris, Irish Cultural Center, Arizona State Art Museum, ASU Ceramics Research Center and Desert View Theatre.

Dr. Schmitt's research has led her to meet with curators at the Louvre Museum and D'Orsay Museum (Paris), National Gallery of Art (Dublin), Calouste Gulbenkian Museum (Lisbon), Museum of Modern Art (New York City), Guggenheim Museum (New York City), Metropolitan Museum of Art (New York City) and the Heard Museum (Phoenix, Arizona). A fine art photographer, she has exhibited her artwork in New York City, Los Angeles, Phoenix and Paris. Her photography illustrates all five of her books.

Photograph by D.C. Larue.

ROSARY O'NEILL, PHD, is a senior Fulbright drama specialist and winner of nine Fulbright awards, including five to study Edgar Degas in Paris. She has published nineteen plays with Concord Publishers (Samuel French Publishers), including *Degas in New Orleans* and *Marilyn/God*, and has published six play/screenplay anthologies, three novels and seven books. She coauthored screenplays with Dr. Rory Schmitt about Kate Chopin, Edgar Degas and the Baroness of Pontalba in New Orleans, and these are currently being optioned as films.

Her other books include *New Orleans Carnival Krewes* (for which she was keynote speaker at the International Carnival Conference, University of Cologne) and *The Actors Checklist*, used as a master text in schools nationwide. Her plays have been performed in Germany, France, Russia, Georgia and England. She has been a visiting scholar at Cornell University, The University of Cologne, University of Bonn and the Irish Cultural Center in Paris. She has received artist residencies at the Norman Mailer Institute; National Arts Club, NYC; the Arthur Seelen Theatre, New York; Virginia Center for the Creative Arts; and the Tyrone Guthrie Center in Ireland.

The founder of Southern Rep Theatre, New Orleans, Dr. O'Neill has received invitations to and sponsorships from American Embassies in England, France, Georgia, Russia and Hungary. She is a professor emerita at Loyola University, New Orleans, and a member of the Playwrights Division of the Actors' Studio in New York City. She has been celebrated worldwide with residencies at Harvard University; Sorbonne University; the American Center, Paris; and the American Academy in Rome.

Her biggest honor is writing with her daughter.